Invisible Woman

Ika Hügel-Marshall

Invisible Woman

Growing up Black in Germany

translated by
Elizabeth Gaffney

Continuum
New York   London

2001

The Continuum International Publishing Group Inc
370 Lexington Avenue, New York, NY 10017

The Continuum International Publishing Group Ltd
The Tower Building, 11 York Road, London SE1 7NX

Printed in the United States of America

Library of Congress Cataloging-in-Publication Data

Hügel-Marshall, Ika, 1947–
   [Daheim unterwegs. English]
   Invisible woman : growing up black in Germany / Ika Hügel-
Marshall; translated by Elizabeth Gaffney.
      p. cm.
   ISBN 0-8264-1294-7 (alk. paper)
   1. Hügel-Marshall, Ika, 1947– . 2. Women, Black—Germany
—Biography. 3. Race discrimination—Germany. 4. Germany
—Race relations. I. Title.

HQ1625.H84 A3 2001
305.48'896043'092—dc21
[B]
                                                    00-060185

Poem by May Ayim, *blues in Schwarz und weiss*, Berlin 1997

For my mother and father

For Dagmar

I would like especially to thank Dagmar Schultz, who stood by my side all along and encouraged me to write this book. I credit her faith in me for its realization.

Hearty thanks also go to Gloria I. Joseph, who devoted much time, at the beginning of the writing process, to constructive and stimulating discussion.

Thanks to Bettina Schäfer, who was the first to hold the manuscript in her hands and gave me both important advice and courage, and to Ekpenyong Ani, for the conversations and the candor with which she edited the manuscript.

And particular thanks to Jani Pietsch, my editor. Our work together has been a pleasure.

distant connections

. . . I know
his dark fingers
on my hand
know
the bright trails they
leave on my skin
shadowkisses on the way

distant connections
connected distances
between continents
at home on the way . . .

—May Ayim

Invisible Woman

IT HAPPENED AGAIN just the other day: Berta burst through the door with a long-awaited letter from her father in her hand, and I was reminded of how much I wanted to find my father. I'd have liked to see him once, from a distance, no more. I had his name and an old address on a scrap of paper, but that was all. I'd been told that wasn't nearly enough information to track down a person in the United States. I didn't even know if he was still living. The idea that I might not find him alive, only his grave-stone, actually seemed more plausible to me than the possibility I would ever meet him face to face. I tried to ignore the other possibility—that he might not want to see me, might deny or disown me, even if he were alive—but that anxiety was there, too. At my age, what did I want from a father anyway? Hadn't I survived all those years without him? Men, and therefore fathers, were more or less dispensable as role models—or so the women's movement in my country had led me to believe—and it certainly wasn't worth pining for them. That is what the women's movement taught me. How, then, could I wish for a father? There are many people who have never known their fathers, and some who say they don't feel they missed out on anything—on the contrary, they hardly noticed the lack.

My father is black, and for that reason I could not share such feelings. The color of my skin binds me to him. I long believed that bond wasn't strong enough to justify my missing him or undertaking the arduous process of finding him.

Germany is my homeland. I've never learned to love it, but I can have no other homeland, no other country nor language. I know my father could never provide me that. Indeed, the very word *father,* so commonly invoked, triggers a sharp pain in me every time I hear it. But I do want to know who I am.

To be black is to be betrayed. For me, being black has meant that people treat me with loathing and indifference. How, then, could I ever have put the thought of my father aside, how could I have avoided him, when the mistrust and rejection were there every day to remind me?

What would I have said to my father, if I'd met him?

They called you *nigger* and my mother *nigger-whore. Black bastard* was the phrase for the likes of me. Not worthy of living, diseased in body and mind, sterilized by the Nazis, locked up in work camps and murdered in death camps. Because we were not Aryan. Dad, it was a long time before I knew your true name.

What would I have said to my father if I'd met him?

I don't want you for a father, because no one wanted me. I was born in Germany of a white mother but never fully arrived in this land. And it's your fault, the fault of your black skin, that I was unwanted in my homeland.

What would I have said to my father if I'd met him?

I am your daughter. I grew up here, in Germany, among whites. I went to kindergarten, to school, I got a degree, I work, but in the eyes of most Germans, I do not exist.

What would I have said to my father if I'd met him?

I am German, you African-American. I am a member of a white German society that wants no part of me, that discriminates against me, that locks me out, that denies me, and that permits blacks to be publicly hunted and struck down.

What would I have said to my father if I'd met him?

I am part of you. I'm your daughter. I've missed you.

MY MOTHER AND I were born in the same small town in Bavaria, she in 1925, I in 1947. She was tall and slim back then, with brown hair and blue eyes, the youngest of eleven children of a respectable working-class family. Her father died when she was ten. At fourteen, she was already working as a housekeeper in a residential section of Munich, although she had been a good student. Because of finances, further schooling was not an option for her.

On September 12, 1944, when the so-called Fraternization Ban was announced, my mother was nineteen. According to this regulation of the occupying armies, Allied soldiers were strictly forbidden from visiting German homes, accompanying Germans to dance halls, sporting events or other public functions, and from marrying German women. All allied contact with Germans was rigorously overseen. These measures were implemented in an attempt to protect the Allied forces from the populace of a nation that had instigated a murderous war. Any contact between the occupying forces and German citizens was considered dangerous and raised suspicions of espionage. It was to be avoided at all costs. Soldiers were constantly forewarned, in print and on the radio, against such fraternization, especially with women or girls. The withholding of friendly contact was also intended to remind Germans of their responsibility for the crimes of their fascist government.

The Fraternization Ban had further implications for the African-American soldiers of the U.S. Army. The inherent racism of the army conformed with the prevailing prejudices of the Germans. Thus, even in the absence of the Allied ban on fraternizing with the enemy, the racism of the Germans would have prevented black soldiers from mixing with German society. In a sense, then, there was a double-ban in place against the black G.I.s. For once their fellow Allies and the Germans agreed on something: discriminating against blacks. Regardless of this, black American soldiers in Germany adhered as little as their white compatriots to the rules of the ban. In fact, they were known to be especially kind to children and generous in distributing any excess cigarettes, food, or clothing available to them.

In May, 1945, after the war in Europe was over, the rules forbidding soldiers from being in the company of Germans were relaxed, and in October, 1945, all but two of the regulation's provisions were lifted: those against visiting German households and marrying German women. German women who subsequently entered into relationships with American soldiers were called *Ami* (American) *whores* or *Ami sweethearts* by other Germans; those who had contacts with black soldiers were called *nigger whores*.

My parents met in 1946, when my mother was almost twenty-one years old. They saw each other in secret, since after the war just as before, their bi-racial relationship was considered immoral by Germans, a violation of racial purity. Now and then, when they had the courage, my parents went out for walks in the park. *Hey, Ami sweetheart. Nigger whore!* Who would choose to endure being called such things in public? And so eventually they began to meet at a friend's house, and they continued to meet, always at the same place, for eight months. They hid themselves away from family and outside world, but every time they

18

parted, they had to leave their happiness and passion behind. My father was twenty-eight and a corporal. In November, 1946, after he recovered from an illness, the army sent him back to the U.S.

Both of them knew my mother was pregnant at the time, but she had no idea he was being restationed until after he was gone.

I was born in March, 1947. My arrival was quietly, anxiously celebrated within my mother's family, but the rest of society had long since made up its mind to exclude me and my mother from the fold. When I was one, my mother married a white German man, and a year later, my younger sister was born. The next five years of my life were relatively trouble-free. We grew up the same way other children did. There was always enough to eat—though no more. We slept in our parents' bedroom. We were a family, even if I always knew my father wasn't really my father. I was aware that people whispered behind their hands when my mother and I went out shopping and that there was something about me that was different from other children. There was only one world, one culture—the white one—and that is the world I was born into. No black culture existed, and I had no black father, no black grandmothers, no black siblings, nor black neighbors in my environment. There was only one reality, one truth. Everyone was white, and all children looked exactly like their parents. And so I imagined that I must be white, too—what else could I be? It was a long time before I really looked into a mirror. In those days, though I understood that there were good and bad things and friendly and unfriendly people, I hadn't yet learned to divide the world into black and white. I saw no reason in the world that I wouldn't be able to grow up with my white mother in my white family and be perfectly happy.

On March 19, 1952, seven years after the war ended and a few days after my fifth birthday, the following article appeared in a German newsmagazine under the headline "What Will Become of the 94,000 Occupation Babies?"*

"This problem has been cast by the leadership party (the Christian Democrats) as primarily a problem of the Occupation. But it is not just a German problem—it has become an international one, and will expand right along with the numbers of peacekeeping forces, just as long as the soldiers of one nation are stationed in the territories of another. At this time, the number of occupation babies is roughly 94,000, including about 3,000 children of mixed race. The numbers have recently tapered off to some extent, but even so, such statistics must give a nation like Germany pause . . ."†

I was five years old and had no idea that for most of the people in my country, I would never grow up—I would remain an occupation baby forever.

"Particular humanitarian and racial problems are presented by one subset of these occupation babies, the 3,093 children of mixed Negro blood. 1,941 of these children live with their mothers; 388 live with their mothers and extended families; 450 are in foster care and 314 are living in institutions. Three hundred fifty are totally without family connections.

* *Das Parlament*, March 19, 1952.
† Ibid.

Of the children in foster and institutional care, 363 still have connections with their mothers.

"A total of 362 colored fathers continue to participate in raising their children. Sixty-eight support their children from outside Germany. Twenty of the Negro fathers went to France after completing their military service, and married the German women or girls they impregnated in that country. The responsible authorities at the appropriate agencies and the department of children's services have long deliberated over what the fate of these mixed-race children should be. Among other concerns there is the fact that they are ill suited to the climate here. It has been suggested that it would be better for these children to relocate them to the homeland of their fathers."

I was five years old and had no idea that the name my mother had given me meant nothing to other people. They would call me *Negermischling*—mixed-race Negro, instead.

"The solution to the problem of these mixed-race children is of great concern to us, as they are detested by Europeans and blacks alike. The inner conflict that characterizes the life of the Mischling *is unmistakable. The child rebels in the face of the contempt it perceives. Part of the* Mischling, *though it may have learned to live like a European, always remains morally corrupt and of bad character."*

I was five years old and had no idea that I presented the people of my country with a moral and humanitarian problem.

"The beginning of their school years is, for Mischling *children, more than just the onset of a new stage of life. This is*

21

the time when they step from the relative isolation of their
previous existence and into a new arena, in which the color
of their skin makes them stand out. Some exhibit behavioral
problems. Those experienced with children will be aware of
how intolerant children can be of anything that falls outside
the norm. Parents, teachers and indeed all of us have a par-
ticular duty in this regard. . ."

I was five years old and had no idea it would turn out
not to be I who presented problems for others but they
who presented them for me.

After eight months of primary school, I was sent to a
Christian children's home far away from where my
family lived. The home was administered by the
Pentecostal Society and the Independent Protestant
Association. As grounds for my institutionalization,
the Youth Services Department cited expected problems with my personal and professional development
if I remained with my family and grew up in the small
town where I was born.

"This is no reflection on your abilities as a mother,
Frau Popp. But surely you know how people are in
small towns, how they talk. Please permit me to give
you some very sound and serious advice—and please
recall that I am the director of Youth Services here and
in charge of such things. In short, I urge you to let your
daughter go. It's the right thing. Send her to a place
where she can grow up without the burdens she would
face here. People can be hateful and mean. Believe me,
the best thing for both of you would be to place her
where she'll be spared contact with such people. She'll
never amount to anything if she stays here with you, in

22

this town. Trust me. It's for the best, and you do want the best for your daughter, don't you? You love her don't you, Frau Popp?"

Every time Herr Siebert from Youth Services comes to visit, I hide, crouching in some corner of the cellar or crawling beneath the woodpile behind the house. The first time he met me, he greeted me by stroking my hair, as if we were well acquainted. He gave me chocolates and asked if I had playmates and whether my mother liked them. I've never seen him act that way with my sister or any other children. He never strokes their hair, gives them chocolate or asks them questions, and the next time he comes, I yank my hand from his tight grasp, throw his candy on the floor and run from him. I don't want to answer his questions. Perhaps it's because I've heard my grandmother tell him, more than once: "Take your hands off my granddaughter, please. And give your bonbons to another child. We have plenty of our own here."

I have no idea at this point that my interaction with Herr Siebert and my grandmother's reaction to him will leave such lasting impressions on me, impressions I will only later be able to understand.

"Herr Siebert, tell me this: How am I to explain to my child that the best thing for her would be to go away from me, to leave home? Of course, I want the best for Erika. I can't change other people. Of course I'm afraid, and sometimes I don't know how the child will bear all she'll have to. If the home is the best place for Erika and they'll truly take good care of her there, then I suppose I do want her to take this difficult step. But tell me, how am I to explain to a six-year-old child that it would be better to grow up without her mother?"

"Frau Popp, it is for the best. She's got no future in this town. When she's older, she may become emotionally unstable and she'll certainly be considered free game for the men. She'll end up having children out of wedlock, become an alcoholic and God knows what else. Is that what you really want? And please don't forget, Frau Popp, that you have another daughter. If you keep Erika here, you'll be endangering her development, too. When it comes down to it, it was your decision to bring another *Negermischling* into a hostile world. And finally, Frau Popp, if you can't make the decision for yourself, I'm afraid we'll have to make it for you.

"Erika?" my mother calls. "You like playing with other children, don't you?"

"Oh, yes!"

"And would you like to travel to another city for a few weeks to stay at a house full of children? Just for six weeks, and then I'll come pick you up."

"Okay," I say, although the words, *Just for six weeks and then I'll come pick you up* have something vaguely threatening about them. Something frightening. I heard doubt and trepidation in my mother's voice. It sounded more like she was pleading with them than arranging a wonderful opportunity for me.

GOD'S LITTLE ACRE *Children's Home* is written in large black letters on a white ground. The sign, which hangs prominently above the entrance, is legible from a long way off. Herr Siebert, my mother, and I are received by a reserved but not unfriendly nun, Sister Hildegard. My mother and I are tired from our long train ride. Later in the evening, we are brought to a small room and served a meager supper. On the way down the hall, we pass a door though which children's voices can be heard. I want to go in, but the small, plump nun with the brown hair grasps my hand tightly and tells me, "You can play with the other children in the morning, when you've gotten some rest." From the very first, I can't stand her. I don't like the way she holds onto me.

Before I fall asleep, I hear my mother repeat *just for six weeks, then I'll come and pick you up*. The next morning the two of us eat breakfast alone, and then I'm taken to the room where I heard the other children. It's the refectory.

"Gerti, Hans, Peter, Annelise—go play with Erika outside. Show her the courtyard and the garden."

It's wonderful, but at some point, overflowing with excitement and the desire to share it, I look up for my mother. I want to tell her how much fun I'm having playing with the children here. I look but cannot find her anywhere.

"What are you looking around like that for? Go wash your hands. Your mother will be back soon enough," Sister Hildegard tells me and sends me to the washroom. After I've done as she says, I go back to playing with the children, but I'm distraught. At supper, when my mother has still not resurfaced, I am overtaken by a feeling of panic. I leap up from the table, run down the long hall, past the kitchen, and am on my way upstairs to the room where my mother and I spent the night when a strong hand yanks me back. "Stop right there! What do you think you're doing, just getting up like that and running off? You will turn around and return to your place at once."

Sister Hildegard drags me behind her all the way back to the table. My wrist hurts. I'm crying from fear and anxiety. Again and again, I try to get up from my seat, but now my slightest movement causes her to press me firmly and unsympathetically back down against the chair rungs.

"Mama, where are you? Why can't you hear me? Mama, why don't you come? Where are you?" I cry, but she doesn't hear me. When I don't stop crying, Sister Hildegard finally grabs a black gym shoe she seems to have at the ready for just this purpose, pulls down my underpants in front of all the other children and beats me with it.

"Stop your endless screaming, you miserable little bastard! Your mother can't hear you, no matter how hysterically you cry. She left on a train first thing this morning."

I am taken, sobbing, to my room. I can't breathe. My every whimper, however quiet, is met with further blows, and at some point I no longer feel anything but the tears burning as they run down my cheeks.

Where is she? Why didn't she come to say, "Goodbye, be good, I'll see you soon"? Sister Hildegard sits by my bed and waits until I fall asleep from exhaustion. Every night thereafter, I lie awake in my bed,

26

rolled into a ball with the covers pulled over my head and cry for hours. *I'll come and get you soon. You like to play with other children, don't you? It's just for six weeks.* Over and over I recall her promises to me. I want to run away, but where would I go? I have no idea how far I am from home, but I know the train ride was a long one. I would never make it on foot. And it doesn't seem possible to escape from the home at all, with Sister Hildegard on the lookout.

Time passes, and I don't know for sure whether six weeks are up. I am so afraid of the beatings that come whenever I say something wrong or ask a question that I'd rather keep silent than ask. Worst of all, it slowly occurs to me, somewhere deep down, that I will no longer be welcome, that I cannot go home. But I don't ask questions—maybe out of fear that I wouldn't be able to bear the answers.

Curled up in a ball, my arms and legs twisted against my body, I sit with my back pressed up against the old wall. It's quiet all around me, frightfully quiet. Screaming won't help. Running won't help. I've been forgotten. I've been left behind, here at this wall, in this strange place. Why? Because the farewell would have been too painful for mother and daughter alike? To forget something is to have no memory of it. To exclude it from the rest of society. I am seven years old and I stand up and wipe the tears from my face.

Time passes, forcing me to come to terms with life at the home. Gradually, the daily rhythms of the place become my reality. For a time, I am uncertain if my entire life before the home was a dream, or whether perhaps my life at the home is the dream. Everything has changed, and I change too. I have chores: scrub the floors daily, wash the dishes, peel the potatoes, weed the garden, iron, darn socks. There is nothing to read here. I can't find a single book that's not one of four separate editions of the Bible. There are not enough toys for all the children, and presumably no money to buy more. I play with what is there, collecting leaves, twigs, rocks, empty jam jars, packs of matches, paper bags, moss, clumps of dirt. I play by myself for hours at a time, building things, utterly absorbed in my solitary games, my toys as worthless as I am. And in this way, I construct a fantasy world that has meaning only for me, a world that cannot be taken away from me. No one teaches me everyday tasks such as how to write and mail a letter, how to shop, to cook or even to make a telephone call. We receive no allowance at the home, and if my mother didn't send me an article of clothing or two every now and then, I wouldn't know what it is to own anything. We dress according to a strict code. We eat what appears on the table, whether we can stomach it or not. Sometimes I can't and, forbidden to get up during meals for any reason, I am sick at the table. When this happens, my hands are tied behind my back to prevent me from striking out and I am force-fed my vomit, spoon by spoon. This happens more than once.

The course of our days at the home is prescribed down to the minutest detail. At 6:30 A.M., we are awakened by a loud voice shouting: *Rise and shine! No sleepy heads! Up up! Out of your beds!* Although we are permitted just enough time to wash our faces and brush our teeth, I dawdle. I am always the last. I enjoy being last. It's the only way I can get even a few moments to myself.

You again! Can't you ever be ready to go when everyone else is? This is not some hotel, you know. Quite aside from the fact that I've no idea what a hotel might be, I don't mind being last at all. The stolen minutes by myself in the washroom when no one is watching me are worth all the scoldings they bring upon me. For breakfast we have Caro breakfast drink, bread, butter, and jam. We get more bread with jam to take with us to school and, very rarely, liverwurst.

I walk to school alone. The other children from the home attend a special school for those with learning disabilities. Along the way, in the morning, I often dream up ways to wangle some of the marvelous snacks I know my classmates will have in their schoolbags. My jam-bread is so pathetic that no one would ever trade me, but I do sometimes manage to enjoy their delicacies. The unspoken rule at school is that no one is allowed to discriminate against me because of my skin color. When they do it anyway, I sometimes suggest that rather than having me tattle to the director, they give me their sandwiches. Thus, maybe once a week or so, I end up tossing my own food in the garbage in favor of my tormentors' better offerings.

After school I hurry back to the home for lunch, which is the main meal of the day. But before lunch, I must change my clothes. We have school clothes, everyday clothes, and Sunday clothes, and I hate all of them. They are all second hand, worn and out of style. I'm forbidden to wear long pants, because I'm a girl. Our nylon shirts are stiff and scratchy, our skirts too long and binding, and I'm uncomfortable wearing them. I'd like to strip them off and never put them back on. My favorite dress was a bright blue one that my mother didn't pack for me, as it was getting small, and I've grown even more since then. Nothing I had when I arrived here fits anymore. Once a year, all the children at the home line up and trade in our shoes for larger ones older children have outgrown, but often there is no pair large enough for me, and I end up walking around with my toes jammed into a pair so small they hurt. On the way home from school, I take my shoes off and put on a pair of slippers hidden in my bag—a gift from my mother. I ignore it when people on the street call out: *Hey, girl, you're still wearing your slippers! Where do you kids get your crazy ideas? Better watch out or one day you'll go off to school without your head.* The slippers are comfortable. That's all that matters to me, and as far as heckling goes, it's not so bad. It doesn't go on for long.

After the main meal of the day, the younger children are sent for their naps and the older ones are allowed to read the Bible. I do my homework by myself, though I'm never left unsupervised. Afterward, there are two or three hours of free time before supper. At eight o'clock sharp the day comes to an end and all is quiet in the home. The weekend routine is different. At 10:00 A.M. we have Sunday school, where we memorize stories from the Bible; at noon we return to the home for lunch and then we go out, en masse, for a stroll. If the weather's bad, we're allowed to listen to the radio in the playroom. On no occasion are we allowed to venture further than five miles from the home, and in winter we are hardly allowed out at all. At school, I overhear classmates talk about skating excursions. They often meet at a lake just across the way from the home, and I watch them enviously from the window. I am not allowed to join them. The children from the home are allowed to go to the lake, but only as a group, under the supervision of several nuns, and because I'm ashamed to have my classmates see me in that context, I never go at all, though my grandmother has given me a pair of skates for Christmas. One day, a storm leaves the entire world sheeted in a thick layer of ice, and I am overjoyed at the unexpected opportunity and teach myself to skate on the frozen-over surface of the road. I finally get to show off this new skill when one of the nuns takes us on a skating trip to another lake, somewhat further away, where it's unlikely I'll run into anyone from school.

I teach myself many things. At school, I'm the first in my class to learn to swim by myself, and my teacher gives me a pencil case as a prize, but at the home, no one notices my diligence or ambition. The sisters don't notice if I bring home prizes or good grades, though they do when the others have successes. Sister Hildegard sits us down in a circle when the report cards come and reads them aloud, praising those who have worked hard or done well. My grades fluctuate from average to good, but regardless of what they actually are, Sister Hildegard only asks me, "Why don't you work harder, Erika? Look at the others' grades. They do their work, behave nicely, and bring home A's. You should be ashamed of your grades. But then we never expected much from you. And now quit your blubbering! You ought to have been so concerned before, when it would have done you some good."

"But my school is much harder than theirs. Why do you have to compare my grades to theirs?"

"If you want to transfer to the special school, all you have to do is say so. Actually, I'm surprised you haven't ended up there already. That's where your kind belongs."

31

Miserable and confused, I go to the bathroom and look at myself in the mirror. I am torn in two. I want so badly not to be what I am. Just for one day, couldn't I be white, too? Perhaps on report card day?

I always go home for a couple of weeks during summer vacation, but I never speak about my life at the home. I don't tell them how badly it's going or how much I want to be allowed back home. Everytime I say good-bye at the end of the visit, my mother tells me, "Soon you'll come home for good, Erika," but she never makes good on her promises. My trust in her is gone. Even so, I can't feel anger or hostility toward her—she's the only person there is who loves me at all and the only person I love. Years will pass before I'm able to tell her about the brutality and mistreatment I suffered at the home and all the things that befell me for which she never took responsibility.

I have no resources to help me develop pride in myself. Why would I be proud? What of? I learn other things instead, like: *You're stupid. Blacks are worthless, regardless of their experience or abilities.* I learn that whites are not to be trusted. They know just how to manipulate me because they understand exactly what they're working with.

Where is there a black face I can look into without seeing something wrong, something laughable, something suspicious?

Who has prepared me to be discriminated against, to be treated as other?

Who fears for me and for all the injury whites will do to me?

The Art of Survival I

How can I recognize that I am loathed for my blackness and that I will not be afforded an equal chance in
life without also giving up completely?
How can I manage to be human when I'm neither
loved nor wanted?
How can I make it through without having tools to
deal with all that? How can I be strong when I never
get an opportunity to recognize my own strength?
How can I make my way through the world standing
upright, when the way is so difficult to tread?
How can I prevent whites from building themselves
up on the basis of my oppression?
How can I make the impossible possible, the unbearable bearable?

I AM TEN and a half years old and completely alone. I keep to myself much of the time, hiding away in some corner, quietly playing my harmonica and dreaming of home. Despite much talk of community, there is no community at the home that I could take part in or belong to. Nor is there any way out of there. All doors are closed. The people who live nearby the home are unfriendly to us. If I ever pause and try to be helpful to any of them in any way, they reject me. *No, thanks. I'll take care of that. Why don't you run along back to the home, now. Do they know you're out here running free in the streets?* It's not just me: all the children from the home are looked at askance (they can spot us right off by our clothes) and no one wants anything to do with us. We are different, and I am the most different of all.

"Oh, that poor child. It's not really her fault she is what she is. It's the mother that should have known better. How could a person be so mean as to bring a child into the world, knowing full well the child's entire life will be a problem? Really, the mother must be a primitive person, or she wouldn't have been keeping company with some Negro. It's clear as day that the daughter will turn out to be just as immoral and licentious as the mother."

I often hear the sisters whisper such things to each other as they make their nightly dormitory rounds. Much of their conversations go over my head, but I understand what they're saying about my mother and I therefore know that they don't know her or anything about her.

When I was with my mother and we went in to town to shop, people would point and say, *There go the nigger whore and her little black bastard daughter.* At those times my mother would hold my hand tighter and stand up taller. I do love her. She could easily have done what so many mothers of Afro-German children did and given me up at birth, but she didn't. She did all she could to make both of us—herself and me—secure in our existences. I knew subconsciously from an early age that she, too, was reviled and derided because she had had me. I knew that she had in some way sacrificed her standing in the community on my behalf. Though her sacrifice was not something she ever explicitly made me aware of, it created a powerful bond between us. She tried not to let me sense the enormous burden my existence placed on her life. Indeed, as long as I was with her, I felt treasured and cared for. My mother taught me to sing beautiful lullabies. It wasn't a lot to build a life on, but that was what I had, and I made do.

Then there was my grandmother. She was there for me, cared for me, played with me, and protected me from adults and children alike. I was her granddaughter, and she never shrank from being seen with me in public. Every day, while my mother was at work, she came over and took care of our household—the shopping, the cleaning, and me. When, occasionally, jibes were tossed her way or mine because of who I was, she never let them go unanswered. She refused to be insulted. She wore her smooth, dark brown hair parted in the middle and pulled back in a tight bun. She had brought eleven children of her own into the world, and to me she was the dearest, most courageous grandmother in the world.

Every Monday she went into the woods to collect brush and deadwood for our fireplace. She would load up her cart and wheel it back to the house. When she arrived, she always had a little treat of some sort for me—a candy, a penny, a sugar lump—and as much as possible, she took me along when she went to her friends' houses or the houses of her other children and grandchildren. She let me know that I was her favorite grandchild, and I suffered greatly when she died at ninety years of age.

The richness of my first seven years continues to be a source of strength for me today, but in the years immediately afterward, I had no other source of strength whatsoever. I was always alone.

I never stopped loving my mother, no matter what awful things the nuns said about her. I swore to myself that I would never believe the words of anyone who had told my mother: "It's not a child you've brought into this world—it's a monster—and the little bastard will never be anything more than just that." As far as I was concerned, the sisters could take their hateful and poisoned words and shove them.

APRIL, 1957. I LOOK out at the great gray station wagon that has come to take me, Sister Hildegard, and another woman from the home called Aunt Gertrude, to Hamburg, where I will have the Devil exorcised from me.

Sister Hildegard called me into her office yesterday to tell me about it.

"Tomorrow you'll be going with Aunt Gertrude and me to Hamburg. You want to be a good girl, don't you? Well, we all know you have an unnatural hussy for a mother, and that she let some Negro have his way with her. This was a very grave sin, and it means that your blood is impure. You have a great deal of Devil in you, child, but we're going to take you to Hamburg tomorrow and pray together that you might be made good and pure. Now, be an obedient child and write down all your sins on a piece of paper for me."

I sit quietly and write: *I am ill-bred, disorderly, and rude. I talk back. I do not comb my curly hair neatly or smoothly enough. I do not work hard in school; all I want to do is play with the other girls. I do not fall asleep promptly at bedtime. I am loud. I do not like to hold hands with the other children when we go out for walks. I am lazy, I lie, and when I pray, I ask God for the wrong things.*

I'm sick of the constant praying here—morning, noon, and night, and four or five times on Sundays. I've been sick of it for a long time. I don't expect my prayers to be answered. After all, I'm still here, despite the huge number of times I've prayed to go back to my mother. In order to give the impression that I'm a diligent, devout girl, I often retreat alone to the dormitory.

But when I'm there, I don't pray, I take out paper and pencil and draw or write little poems. In this way, on paper, I'm able to express things I dare not speak aloud. I fold my poems and drawing up into neat little squares and hide them beneath my mattress, but one day they are discovered.

"What is this garbage, why have you written it, and whom exactly do you intend to read your dreadful scribblings?"

"No one. I just wrote it," I say in a frightened whisper.

Sister Hildegard takes my pages and rips them into hundreds of tiny sheds before my eyes, then commands me to pick them up and throw them in the trash.

We get into the car. At this hour of the morning, the streets are still completely empty, and it seems we are the only ones going anywhere. I am apprehensive but at the same time a little excited to have been singled out to go on this trip with Sister Hildegard. Sitting so close to her in the car only increases my anxiety. She is a great, fat woman and wears a long gray dress with a habit of the same color that entirely covers her hair. I've never seen her hair. Today, she has her arm around my shoulders. Why, when the rest of the time she only uses it to beat me? I don't like it. Her overtures are unpleasant, and I don't trust her affection. Also, I am hot, and her closeness is oppressive. There is not enough room in the car. I need more space. I can barely breathe. Or I wish that at least she wouldn't press so closely against me, but she responds not at all to my squirming attempts to free myself from her embrace. At last, hours later, the car stops and we get out—what a relief. The air is cool and it's raining lightly. Then suddenly the drizzle turns to a downpour. Sister Hildegard does up the front of my coat, opens her umbrella and takes me by the hand. The gravel walk is wet and slippery. Some distance from the street stands a white-washed brick house, where a group of well-dressed men and women are standing under a large wooden portico at the entry-way, talking. The house seems to be the only building anywhere nearby. All I can see in any other direction are fields and trees. In the distance, I hear a barking dog and the droning of a combine.

"All right, get a move on. There's nothing here worth gawking at. We don't have all day. You should be thinking about what you're going to say when we get inside, not standing around dreaming. Let's go!"

Sister Hildegard's step quickens, and she takes hold of my arm and drags me behind her all the way past the doorway with the people and around to a side entrance. She opens the door and we step into a small room, empty but for a small, brown wooden chair at the center. The windows are closed and I am filled with dread. Across from me stands a tall man dressed in black. Beads of sweat blossom and run down his spongy, bloated face. His eyes bulge, fixing me in a stare that is almost, but not quite, friendly. I'm terrified enough to grab at the long gray skirts of Sister Hildegard for protection, but she bends down, unclamps my fingers and directs me to go to the man.

"Be brave now," she whispers. "Think of your mother and how much she worries about you. You want to be a good girl, don't you? You don't want to cause you mother trouble, do you? And don't you want people to like you?"

"Kneel down at the chair here," says the man quietly, almost gasping, as if he can't get enough air. His hands

41

tremble. He reaches into his pocket, takes out a hand-kerchief, and wipes the corners of his mouth. Slowly, fearfully, I cross to the middle of the room, where the chair is, and kneel before it. He moves toward me with heavy steps and I stand back up, cry out, try to get away from him.

"Come back here!" he bellows. "That door is locked. Nothing will happen to you here. You must not be afraid."

I stand frozen at the door until Sister Hildegard takes me by the shoulders and pushes me back to the chair. She stands behind me and blindfolds me with a brightly pattered cloth.

"Be a brave girl, for once. Your mother will be proud of you."

"Repeat after me, loudly and clearly," says the man in a strong, insistent tone. *"Lord Jesus." "Lord Jesus."* . . . *"Forgive me my sins." "Forgive me my sins."* . . . *"Deliver me from evil." "Deliver me from evil."* . . . *"Satan, I cast you out." "Satan, I cast you out."* . . . *"Purify my black soul." "Purify my black soul."* . . . *"Jesus is my savior." "Jesus is my savior."* . . . *"Jesus is my savior." "Jesus is my savior."*

Eventually, I'm overcome by nausea and chills. My entire body shakes and I vomit on the floor. I don't know where I am or what world this is, what reality. Is it the one I've been living in, which replaced the earlier dream of home, or is it something new? My head spins and I cannot think. I feel weak. Finally Sister Hildegard takes the blindfold off me, wipes my vomit off the floor and opens the window. She says: "You've done it. Your devils have all flown out this window. And now, if you behave yourself and stop talking back and do as you're told, perhaps they'll stay away."

42

For years I suffer nightmares. I'm afraid of myself. I'm afraid of the dark. Everywhere I imagine little black devils: behind the cellar door, in the basement, under my bed, in my book bag in the morning before school, at school anytime something goes awry, when I am alone. I'm afraid the devils will sneak up and capture me, torture me and throw me in a deep, dark grave. I am ten years old, and I'm riddled with guilt. I hate the color of my skin. From this time on, I have no greater desire than to be white.

It takes me a long time to absorb that I am perceived as different from everyone around me, and a long time to absorb that this difference is something bad. But eventually I do absorb it. It doesn't help when the occasional lady on the street, who calls herself my "auntie," gives me a bit of chocolate and says, "you poor, poor thing." My otherness is irrefutably proven whenever I am impolite or naughty, I am called *little devil* or *unmanageable creature* and told that I lack intelligence, I'm a creature of base instinct. "That's the Negro in her coming out," they say. I don't know what to make of these statements at first, though it's clear that they're saying something bad and it has to do with me. Certainly there are a few people in my life who are kind to me and soothe the hurts I suffer, but, for the most part, I have no choice but to believe what I hear people say about me. How would I know whether what they say is true? Who could I ask?

Every morning, I look in the mirror, but no matter how hard I look, I can't see what's wrong with me. I have long, dark, curly hair pulled back in a pony tail. I've got dark brown eyes, long legs and I'm one of the tallest in my class. But I must be ugly. Otherwise why would

43

people express such disgust when they look at me? Otherwise they wouldn't have taken me to have my devils driven out. Otherwise they wouldn't scrub my skin with a vegetable brush until it bleeds, just to prove to the other children that the color is real and I am not, after all, just one of those chocolate candies called "nigger kisses."

There must be something awful about the way I look, or they wouldn't single me out for the hardest and most frequent beatings. I wouldn't be the only one whose hair was called "obstinate Negro hair." I wouldn't be the only one they never took in their arms, never patted on the back, never said looked pretty, and simply never loved the way they loved the other children.

At home, when I was with my mother, at least everyone in town knew me. The neighbors talked to me and sometimes invited me to their houses for a piece of cake or a glass of juice, just as they did the other children. Everyone knew one another. It was a small town, and the effects of the war were still being felt there. Nearly all of the townspeople struggled just to survive. They were starting over and managing to cope. Maybe that brought them together. I was comfortable within my family—I felt I had a home. It was one of my jobs to collect fresh milk from the nearby dairies, and farmers always had time for us children. I was out and about all day long with my friends, never bored or lonely. Often we lost ourselves in our games, forgetting the time until some grown-up called out, *Don't you kids have to go home at some point?* In the mornings, I loved to accompany the postman a little way along the road, carrying his bag. Then I would go down to the bakery for fresh rolls for breakfast. And I loved coming home to Mama, who was always glad to see me.

44

IT IS THE END of my first year away from home, and I begin to get excited as the last day of school draws near and, with it, my first summer holiday. Soon I will see my mother, my grandmother, my sister. Maybe I won't have to come back to the home, maybe never again. But promptly at the end of the vacation, my mother packs my suitcase. My stepfather will be taking me back to the home.

I have no name for my stepfather. He doesn't talk to me. In winter he shovels snow into a bank to make a sled run for me and my sister. He teaches me to ride a bike and to whistle with two fingers. He never strikes me nor deprives me of material things. I like him, but I don't know whether it's because of these things or just because I'm grateful I don't have to be afraid of him. He is never a father to me. How could he be? A white man who fought "honorably" in the army during the war returns after a year in a P.O.W. camp and marries a woman who already has a child born out of wedlock—and on top of that, it's an "occupation baby"—and if that weren't enough, she had the child by a "Negro." That's what everyone is thinking, clicking their tongues, and many don't hesitate to say it aloud. "She ought to be ashamed of herself for the fact that he even married her, that nigger-whore. She's lucky to have gotten such a nice, proper man. She's to be envied. But if I were him I wouldn't take an ounce of responsibility for her bastard daughter."

On Fridays, when the rest of the family goes shopping, I stay home alone beacuse my stepfather doesn't want to be seen with me. He doesn't want people talking about him. Sometimes Mama tries to make me feel better about this by giving me chocolates, but we're poor and with prices going up and up, she can't justify spending money on chocolate. I understand, though. I'm willing to bear my exclusion from the shopping trips. I do it for her. I've sensed that my mother's insistence on including me in the past has jeopardized my having a family at all, a father of any sort.

Once, after she'd had a fight with my stepfather, my mother took my hand and lead me from the house, crying. We walked for hours, neither of us speaking a word. Even now, I can feel her tears on my face. She held my hand firmly and I wished with all my might that I had at least done something bad—stolen something, not finished my homework, sneaked a gulp of honey straight from the pot—so that there were a reason for her tears, so that I could understand why she was crying.

The train arrives, and I must return to the home. My mother stays home with my sister who is two years younger than I am. On the train ride, only the most essential words are exchanged between my stepfather and me. "Would you like something to eat or drink? We're nearly there. You'll be back for another visit during vacation." I sit quietly in my place and struggle not to cry in front of him nor let him see that I'm already homesick. I am not close to him and certainly don't feel safe enough with him to tell him how much I want to live at home, with the family. Now and then I sniffle and cover my face with a tissue in embarrassment.

"Picked up a cold in the last few days, have you?" is all he can say, and I say nothing at all. Insecurity and misery have sealed shut my throat. Maybe he doesn't ask me questions because he's afraid to hear what I'd say.

When we get to the station, he walks me to the bus stop, as has been arranged. He takes my hand to help me up the first high step of the bus.

"Be a good girl," he calls, and I wave to him and keep on waving as long as he's in sight.

They're expecting me at the home. "Well, what's wrong with your eyes?" is the greeting I get. "Looks like you've got a nasty conjunctivitis." And with that Sister Hildegard sends me to my room. Later, freshly washed and dressed in my everyday-wear, I sit down to supper with the other children. They laugh together, whisper in one another's ears and generally behave as if I weren't there. I'm not hungry, and because I won't eat my supper, I'm made to sit alone at a separate table and then sent to bed early. I manage to hold back the tears till I'm lying down. I am hurting, but by now I've learned not to let the others see me cry.

The Art of Survival II

I begin to learn what life is about and not to let the education I receive interfere with my knowledge.

I begin to suspect that the meaning of life may lie in finding a meaning for meaningless suffering.

Painfully, inexorably, I make my way toward the meaning of suffering. I do not give up. And in this way I preserve a certain reverence for and mindfulness of my own suppressed emotions.

In a racist society, to survive is to fight, every moment, every day. What time is left over for tenderness between a white woman and her black child? But it's that very tenderness we both need so badly.

How can I tolerate my mother's desire to be respected within this society, her fear of sending me forth into a racist world?

In my heart, I feel my mother's love and her unexpressed fear—and, close by, her discrimination; she, who is white, must find a way to integrate the hatred and racism of whites into her life, into her survival strategy.

I'M THE ONLY black child at the home. Because of this, the other children dislike me and take a certain pleasure in bossing me around.

Peter is a short, fat boy who stutters. I'm the only one who's patient enough to wait for him to say what's on his mind, but I don't know why I bother to indulge him. He does quite the opposite with me, constantly laying false blame on me and then tattling about it to the nuns. In this way he makes himself their pet, while I am punished for things I haven't even done. I do listen quietly to Peter, but I don't really like him.

Gerti is a bed-wetter. Every morning, under the close scrutiny of one of the sisters, she is made to wash her sheets out and hang them on the clothesline where all can see. She chews her fingernails and at twelve years old still cannot read or write. I am made to spend an hour tutoring her every day, but still she doesn't deign to play with me—I'm too stupid and I smell funny, she says.

Hans is the strongest of all the children. He's four years older than I am, has blond hair and his own scooter. The others tease him for his ears, which stick out from his head like two sails. There is a time when he keeps on stealing my pencil case from my schoolbag every morning. To get it back, I have to grovel at his feet and repeat three times: *I'm a little niglet, a chocolate-covered piglet.* Sometimes one of the sisters interrupts this and puts an end to my humiliation. Often, I leave for school without my pen.

I love to play games, and every once in a while I succeed in getting everyone excited enough about one

49

of my ideas that even Hans, Peter, and Gerti forget whom they're playing with and join in. When we play school, I give them especially difficult problems that I know they won't be able to solve. It's just a game, but it brings me a bit of malicious glee to pay them back in this way for their beastly treatment of me.

There is one thing they'll always have over me, though: they can hurt me in a way I can't hurt them. Laughing at and discriminating against me are socially acceptable, and everyone does it.

It is universally accepted that it is a terrible thing to be black and that blacks are stupid and so on and so forth, and nothing in my daily experience suggests otherwise. What other choice do I have but to accept this evaluation? It's no wonder I try as hard as I can to ignore my blackness, no wonder that my desire not to stand out from the crowd grows ever stronger.

But no matter what I do to blend in, I cannot conceal my blackness fully enough to spare myself the hurtful attitudes of others. I cannot avoid being hurt. I'm still visible.

For this reason, acknowledgment of my pain now becomes crucial to my survival. Every day I feel an urgent need to express the fury that has accumulated in me because of these insults, the fury at having been prevented from learning to see myself as a self-confident member of society.

But what can I do with this fury, which is directed at precisely those people with whom I'm least confident, at those who react to even my slightest expressions of anger by punishing me more? How often do I think to myself: just don't react, don't give them fuel for their fire, don't let them get a foothold that will become the basis for further attacks, and above all, don't take their bait. Be silent, sit quiet, be aware. They're waiting hungrily for me to speak one careless word, to give them some imagined justification for a new assault on me. That is the only way they know of to manage their own helplessness.

At some point I come to understand that whites don't really even need a justification—they strike out at me even without one, and regardless of whether I react or not. All whites are racists. They are racists simply because they—like I myself—have accepted the accepted truth about me. They believe what they've been taught: that blacks are stupid and worthless by nature.

Together, we sing the song of "The Ten Little Niggers." We play a game called "Who's afraid of the black bogeyman?" and the only difference between me and the other children is that I'm expected to glean a lesson about myself in the process.

In my first years at the home, I loved school, but gradually I come to hate it. In the eyes of my teachers, everything I do—especially the difficulties I have in school, but also my successes, achievements, and all that I am proud of—is a function of the color of my skin. When I do well—and sometimes I'm at the top of my class—my teachers ignore it or confuse my work for another student's, doling out praise to that child instead of me. Or they accuse me of cheating. "This isn't really your work, is it? It's not exactly what one would expect from you." My insatiable curiosity and love of learning suffer because I have no chance to demonstrate my knowledge or skills. It is forbidden to speak or to ask questions unbidden, and we are expected to answer every question directly, succinctly, and without hesitation. Digressions of any sort are not tolerated. Imagination is a cause for punishment. Talking to the kid next to you or failing to pay attention bring raps on the knuckles. I feel dead at school, being forced to sit there and just listen all day long.

It's not what I know or don't know or even bad behavior that brings me to the teachers' attention, it's the color of my skin, and I have no power to change that. We all break the same rules against climbing trees, chewing gum, and making noise, but my transgressions are treated differently than the other children's. It's always me whom the teachers lecture: *You should be ashamed of yourself. Your wildness will be the end of you yet. We're not Hottentots living in the bush here, you know. Go comb your hair—you're starting to look like one of them, too!*

Sometimes, if I'm lucky, I'm dismissed like the others with just a few reproachful words or indulged with a smile. But I've learned that even when I'm included in the benevolence extended to others, it doesn't mean I'm their equal.

In Germany, it's in the fifth grade that children are put on the educational tracks that determine their future careers; the academic track leads to attending a *Gymnasium* and going to a university for a master's degree or Ph.D.; the other tracks lead to apprentice programs or technical or professional high schools. At the end of fourth grade, my one sympathetic teacher talks to me about it.

"I know you want to go to the *Gymnasium*, and I think you could do it, but I'm not sure it's a good idea.

52

Even here, the children are so awful to you. It will only get worse there."

"But I want to go. I want to be a teacher."

"Listen, Erika, I've also talked it over with Sister Hildegard, and she's not in favor of it. She has other plans for you."

"Couldn't you try to talk to her again?"

"She's made up her mind. She won't let you. Maybe it's for the best. I do believe she has your best interests in mind."

I believe her because I like her. Her voice is calm and even when she's teaching. The way she pronounces words, they sound freshly made, as if I'd never heard them before. She praises me often and sometimes even holds up my journal in front of the class to show how neat and even my writing is. "I especially like the drawings you've made under some of the poems," she says loudly to everyone and smiles at me with real affection. One day she takes me aside and whispers: "Child, you're going to amount to something. Don't let the others get to you. Defend yourself. Strike back."

I try to defend myself physically, but it's not a successful strategy. No amount of punches I deal can change my feeling that I'm worthless and stupid compared to the others.

As I grow older I don't let anyone beat me up any more, but this just causes the standard critique of me to shift. Now it's: *That's no way for a girl to behave.* And me? I have no faith left in myself. I finally internalize that I'm laughable, negligible. And knowing myself to be a nothing, I then stop defending myself, stop fighting back. I clench my fists in agony and frustration, jam them in my pockets and flee. The desire for respect from the one or two people, like my fourth grade teacher, who would even contemplate respecting me is not nearly enough to counteract the rejection I get from almost all other white people. Nor is the love of my mother sufficient to prevent me from questioning the entire white society I live in.

Where could I have gone, not to be ignored? Who might have talked to me about my skin color and why it made me an outsider? Who could have taught me how to survive in a society that wanted to be rid me?

I'm constantly homesick, but especially so after one of my mother's occasional visits. I have to watch her and my sister board the train, and I am not allowed to join them. I am locked out. I stand on the platform waving and waving, confused, feet rooted in place. If only I had the courage to jump on the moving train. *You'll be coming home for good, soon,* calls my mother from the window, every time, before she disappears. I throw myself to the ground and sob. All I want is to choke on the dust and never get up again, but someone always pulls me to my feet, saying, *Child, child, it's not so bad.* And he or she wipes my tears away and says kind things and helps me straighten out my clothes.

At the home, for every act of disobedience, every word of back talk, every mess made, and even every slouch, a black mark is carefully entered into the record book. Whoever receives more than ten marks over the course of a week is punished. And so it is that once a week I get a beating and am sent to solitary confinement. My hands are bound and I'm dragged up to the narrow

54

room under the eaves, where I must stay for three hours. I sit crouched over because the roof is too low to stand. In summer it is hot and stifling. In winter I freeze, and my chronic cough sets the dust swirling, sometimes so much that I think I will suffocate. But I would rather die that way than call out to let one of the nuns know how frightened I am.

When the beatings are to be administered, the guilty must line up in a row of chairs and wait their turns for the blows they have "earned." One day, I decide that I will not cry out when Sister Hildegard strikes me. I swallow the tears and the pain and try to deflect the full force of the paddle blows with my hand before they land on my behind. I grit my teeth. Every time she swings, my hands shoots back to shield myself. I don't cry. She strikes my hand, hard, ten times or more.

"What's wrong today, Erika? Doesn't it hurt as much as usual? What are you trying to prove?"

She hits me harder and faster, harder and faster, as if she never means to stop. Finally, I can't bear it and fall to my knees, begging her to spare me further.

"Stand up, you. What did you think, that you were so special you could set an example for the rest of them, play the hero? As for the rest of you, your turns are coming up, so you might as well start thinking now about whether you ever want to sit down again."

The knuckle at the base of my index finger is badly swollen, and I'm sick to my stomach from the pain. Sister Hildegard notices the finger and says, "You don't need a doctor—you're the one who's so tough and strong. And anyway, you asked for it." I return to my place in the row of chairs.

55

She always says the same thing: *Next. Pants down. You again. Well, let's see if we can beat the Devil out of you this time.* Every time, I resolve not to show the humiliation I feel, not at being beaten, but at having to bend over with my pants down, at the total violation of privacy.

Far worse than the beatings, though, are the lies I accept as truth: blacks are stupid, backward, primitive, uncivilized. They are unreliable, shifty, dangerous, pitiful.

When Sister Hildegard goes at me with her paddle, she says, *I'm not beating you, I'm beating the Devil inside you.* She refuses to acknowledge her responsibility for my pain. She never says, *Be brave, be strong.* Childhood is when we learn how to understand the world, and the way I learn to estimate my own value at the home will determine how I think and behave for a long time to come. I learn that a lie becomes the truth as soon as someone believes it. I learn from whites that I cannot trust them.

But the most disastrous thing I learn at the home is self-hatred. The nuns systematically go about dismantling my personality, and I help them do it. I despise myself in an attempt to make myself more acceptable to them.

It's the middle of the week, a sultry oppressive day, and I'm lying in bed reveling. One of my dreams has come true: a classmate has invited me to her birthday party. I clap my hands with delight. I don't quite know how to respond to this piece of good fortune. Then the door flies open and Sister Hildegard sweeps in.

"What are you doing lying about in bed? It seems we'll have to put an end to your outrageous behavior by force!"

I leap up from my bed and run from her in fear.

"Don't think you'll get away that easily," she calls after me as I flee down the hall.

That night and every night for six months, I go to bed with my wrists bound together by a thin strip of cloth.

"You want to go to a birthday party, do you? You, of all people, were invited to a birthday party. Well, you'll have to learn how to behave a little better before you can go to other people's houses. What would that girl's parents think of us? You're an embarrassment. I forbid you to go. Do you understand me?"

I say nothing.

"Well, do you? Or has the cat got your tongue, you dirty little pig? We'll see how long you can keep up this silent treatment. Tomorrow is another day, don't you know."

The next day, while the other children are doing their homework, she sends me out to the garden, makes me take off my shoes, and instructs me to hop in circles around an apple tree. For thirty minutes, she watches me hop, not allowing me to stop or rest for a moment nor even to switch feet. *Just do it*, I tell myself over and again, *and no matter what, don't fall down.*

"That's enough," she finally says. "Put your shoes back on. Go on, do it. Chop chop! You're not so slow when it comes to doing certain other things."

It is the first time I can say I feel true fury. I do not put my shoes and socks back on, and that night I do not join the others for supper. When I'm asked questions, I don't respond. Once again, I've done something forbidden, and once again, I have no idea what. I never did find out.

With my hands bound, how can I open my arms to people? How can I reach out my hands to anyone in solidarity, in greeting, in reconciliation?

How can I ever learn to walk on two feet when I'm made to hop on one?

How can I manage not to grow hard when merely surviving is a high-wire act?

When our final exam grades are posted, there's an end-of-year celebration at the intermediate school I now attend, and afterward, a few of us go out to the ice cream parlor near the train station where kids from our school usually hang out. Just as I'm about to get up and head back to the home, Sister Hildegard appears in the ice-cream parlor and marches up to me.

"What on Earth are you doing here? What could you be thinking? I've been standing outside watching you for some time now, and I've seen enough to make me want to spit—to spit on you. Take yourself straight back to the home, right now. And when I return, you and I will sit down and have a talk about your impossible behavior."

I feel the fury rising.

What is so impossible about my behavior? So awful that Sister Hildegard wants to spit on me? What have I done that's so wrong? Nothing different than anyone else.

"Sit down," screams Sister Hildegard. "If I ever, ever again see you hanging around with a boy or a bunch of boys, or if I so much as hear that you have done so, you'll get a whipping you'll never forget. You should be ashamed of yourself, you devil. You'll come to no good soon enough as it is, but now that I see it's already started, I've decided to send you to a boarding school where you'll be trained as a child-care worker. You'll never marry, that's clear enough, and so you'll have to be able to take care of yourself."

"But I don't want to be a child-care worker. I want to be a teacher."

"A career in social work is really your only option. I think you'll be capable of working with young children, though anything beyond that is quite out of the question. And by the way, I couldn't care less what that teacher of yours or anyone else has told you. Why, the very fact that I just caught you running around with a bunch of boys proves that you're incapable of leading a proper life. I'll tell you what will happen: those boys will use you, and you're such a dumb goose you'll fall for their lines. But do you really think anyone would want you for anything more?"

What can I say? I want to spend time with my friends. I want to belong. And, yes, I would like to know how it feels to have someone infatuated with me.

"That's all. In fourteen days you'll be at the boarding school. Now get out of my sight."

AT THE BOARDING school in Düsseldorf-Kaisers-werth I share a room with another girl my age. We've been told to look out for each other. Our room is fairly large, not very cozy but clean and well suited for studying. Some time later, I learn that Susi and I are the only two girls at the school who have grown up in institutions. The others all come from middle-class homes with parents.

The rules are strict at this school, but I'm used to that. Everything must always be in its proper place; everything put on one's plate must be eaten; and there's no talking of any sort allowed at the table. Our rooms must always be immaculate and ready to pass inspection. If there a crease is found in our bed sheets or the coverlet while we're at class, we return to find the entire mattress and all the bedding overturned on the floor. We wear nurse's uniforms—blue dresses with white aprons—and are forbidden to wear our own clothes, except on rare occasions. On Sundays we take walks as a group along the banks of the Rhine under the supervision of the headmistress. There are only a few hours of free time in the entire week, but I wouldn't know what to do with free time if I had it. I've never been on my own among people in a city. I'm sixteen years old, but I don't know a thing about the world. I have never cooked myself a meal or gone shopping. I don't know what the inside of a post office looks like, nor, for that matter, any other office. I've never eaten in a restaurant or sat with a book on a park bench. My skills are limited to writing and arithmetic, ironing and sewing on buttons.

Susi and I become friends. She teaches me everything that sixteen year olds know. We go to the ice cream parlor, to cafés, to the hairdresser, shopping. We get crushes on boys our age, put on lipstick and rate each other on our looks. Susi and I are both outsiders, though in different ways. She is white. When we graduate from our program, she quickly finds a position as a trainee. I do not.

I'm back home at my mother's for weeks, just waiting for someone to offer me a job. Every rejection pushes me further into a state of helpless rage. Finally, I take out paper and pen and write two letters, one to Susi and one to Frau Werner, the headmistress of the boarding school. I pour out everything I'm feeling and ask them for help. My self-confidence is at a low, and every day I'm even more overwhelmed by feelings of hopelessness. The uncertainty of my future is so terrifying that, for the first time in my life, I feel I want to end it all. I want to kill myself. I simply can't stand to watch all my white classmates get positions while I am repeatedly turned down. A week later I receive this letter from the headmistress:

March 20, 1965

Thank you for your letter. I do hope that in the meantime you have realized what a poor impression it makes to let oneself go and to express one's feelings freely. You are old enough at eighteen to have learned to keep yourself together. I do not condemn your attitude, but neither do I approve of it. I wish you'd think of other people, for once. Think of your mother. Have you ever tried to put yourself in her place? Please try to imagine it. I truly pity your mother—think of all she's endured. Surely she does not deserve to have you act this way. Every day she takes on more and more burdens, just in the attempt to provide her children a decent life. Please try to make her happy. And don't forget that you are now enjoying a holiday, while your father, mother and sister are all either working or attending school. It is your job, then, to try to take care of the household. You were here for two years. Now you must take some initiative. Try to see what work needs to be done around the house, and do it. Try cooking. I hope you learned a bit more here than how to boil water and potatoes.

Yours, Frau Werner

I think long and hard about what she has said, even though her letter reveals no trace of sympathy or understanding. A few days later, I'm summoned to the office of Herr Siebert from Youth Services.

"I've heard about the letter you sent to your school, and I had a copy sent to me. Well, all right. Here. Let me give you this, so you can hang yourself—do it right here before my eyes if you want to."

I say nothing as Herr Siebert pushes a thick length of rope across the desk at me. He continues talking. "Just who do you think you are, then? Haven't you ever contemplated how difficult you've made your mother's life, you ungrateful girl? There are so many people on the Earth who are worse off than you. Pull yourself together and have a little patience until someone has a trainee position that's suitable for you. And don't let me hear that you've written any more threatening letters. Act like a normal person. A bit more is expected of a person your age, you know. You're not the only one in the world with problems."

I say nothing. I stand up and take the rope from his desk. He puts out his hand in leave-taking, and to my own amazement I reach out and hang the rope around his neck. "Maybe you need this more than I do," I say and leave his office without turning back. I'm deeply hurt by his words, but yet it is a moment of triumph. I won't give up, certainly not now.

Weeks and weeks pass, and still I'm at home, waiting around for a job. I feel alone and misunderstood. My sister Lisa, unlike me, is growing up well taken care of. She's two years younger and still in school. She was never able to fathom why one day her older sister just wasn't there anymore. We loved each other above all, when we were girls, and we were never able to ask why we were suddenly forbidden from growing up together.

"I never got an answer when I asked why they sent you to the home," she tells me. "You can't imagine what it was like for me not to have you there anymore. I kept calling out for you, looking for you, and every time they'd tell me you were coming home soon. Mama used to run her hands along the edge of your bed, crying quietly so I wouldn't hear. Once she took all the money out of the kitty, packed up our things. The two of us were going to go get you and bring you home. But then Papa came home. She screamed: 'I'll divorce you if you don't let me have my daughter with me!' Then they sent me to my room so I wouldn't hear the rest of it. Later, the doorbell rang and it was Grandma. I was in my room for three hours, and I could hear that Grandma was talking to them in the kitchen, their voices growing loud and then quiet again. I packed up my favorite doll to give you and waited for Mama to come and say she was ready to go. It was dark by the time Grandma came in and told me: 'Your Mama has thought about it and decided to wait till the summer holiday to take you to visit Erika. You can give her your doll then, if you want. Come now, we're having dinner.' For a long time I was afraid they'd give me away, too."

Lisa and I share everything that all siblings share—everything, that is, but a father. He was hers alone.

One Saturday night, we decide to go out to the local disco together. I've never been to a disco. We drink orange juice while Lisa's friends drink beer. They chat and gossip with each other about school, jobs, and what their various friends are up to. I have nothing to say. I know no one and have no idea what I could contribute to the conversation, so I keep quiet. Every once in a while I look to Lisa for help. And then one of the others asks her, in a voice so loud and clear I suspect the entire disco hears it: "So, is she your friend, Lisa?"

My sister sets her glass on the table with a shaky hand and without looking at me, says, "Yeah."

Her *yeah* cuts me to the quick. She's just denied that I'm her sister.

Immediately, though, I suppress the event and begin to search for reasons that she would need to reject me. I take her side. They're her friends—she needs them. She lives here, and I'll be going away again soon—I don't need them as friends. I've learned to understand others without being understood myself; Lisa hasn't. But I forgive her because she's my sister.

That night I lie awake in bed and try to find the words to explain to Lisa what's going on inside me and what I want. It's not easy for me to talk about my father and how much I want to find him, but the next morning I ask her to help me write him a letter. I know my mother has his address on a scrap of paper she has saved in a drawer. Maybe he'll answer me and I'll find that he understands all my woes, even what happened last night at the disco. Maybe he'll agree to see me. Maybe I'll have a father who acknowledges me. Maybe everything will be different. Maybe.

April 5, 1965

My dear Father,
Unfortunately I do not know whether you live or you died. Do you know that you have a daughter with eighteen years, which is ready with her perfection? Why do you not write? Please write me a letter, I hope it will reach you, if you live please write me a letter. I was born on the 13th of March 1947.

I am crazy, worked up for days on end, incredibly, unbearably edgy. I'm terrified he won't respond.

"There's a letter for you."

"Really?"

"I think it's from Susi," my mother says, and I am crushed. I'm so depressed and disappointed, I put Susi's letter aside and don't read it till the following day.

Dear Ika,
Thanks for your very honest letter. I have to say the situation sounds awful. I think you should

66

talk to Frau Werner. The school is ultimately responsible for placing you, either at a home or in a private family situation.

But on the other hand, I wouldn't trust her an inch. It's completely her fault you didn't get the job you applied for here where I'm working. They actually had to close down one of the children's wards because they were so short staffed, and they definitely would have hired you if she hadn't come around and said that you were "different." They only didn't want you because she said you wouldn't fit in.

Have you written to your father yet? If I were you—or if I were myself, I guess—I wouldn't. What do you want from it, what do you think it will accomplish? I don't want to tell you what to do, but maybe you should consider how it will make your mother feel. She's not made of iron—she's as sensitive as you are, though you may not see it. Erika, you always wish people would be nicer to you—what about the opposite, being nice to other people? But I don't mean to moralize. I'm just trying to be helpful. One thing I think is so great about you is the way you don't see any point in rehashing things—you let bygones be bygones. I got that insight from a book, not other people. Hey, guess what? I got my first pay check—96.25 DM—I went right out and bought a book all about love. Maybe it'll help me find some.

Much love, Susi

67

Before I have time to answer Susi's letter, I get back the one I sent to my father. RETURN TO SENDER/INSUFFICIENT ADDRESS is stamped on the envelope, which is postmarked May 21, 1965. I resolve never to write to him again.

When my mother sees how disappointed I am, she tells me about her unsuccessful attempts to find him, just after I was born. Then again in April, 1952, with the help of *The Voice of America—New York 19*, she wrote to the State Department's "lost and found" service in Chicago. A month later she received a letter from the Chicago Police Department.

> Dear Madam,
> With reference to your letter of recent date regarding locating Eddie Marshall, last known address 4959 Prairie Avenue, this city. Officers assigned report that nobody by that name is known at or in the vicinity of above address. In the event he is located here later, you will be notified.

My life goes on without my father.

Three months later, I finally get a position and stay there for a year before I decide I want to take the intermediate school diploma exam that I missed when I was sent to boarding school. I send in all my certificates and the application materials. In response, I receive a letter from the school asking me to explain why I want to get my diploma. A short time later my application is accepted.

I get the call on a Tuesday afternoon. Frau Lehnert, the guidance counselor, asks me to come see her. She has my results on the desk in front of her.

"You've failed, Erika. You're not going to graduate."

She's friendly. She hands me a tissue to wipe my tears and says, "All right now. Let's just see what we can do about this."

At that moment I don't want her to help me. I tell her in a fit of tears, fury and indignation about all my teachers' injustices toward me, how I was always put alone at a table when we did in-class assignments, how they dragged me to the front of the class and humiliated me, laughed at the clothes I wore, criticized my hair and sent me to the bathroom during lessons just to have me comb it into submission. Frau Lehnert says nothing.

I get up and walk toward the door, but then I turn and yell at her: "I'm leaving. All right. I don't give a damn about any of it, but I do know I didn't deserve to fail. I've had it. It's enough. I don't care anymore. But I did work hard, every day. I was always there, raising my hand, but no one ever called on me. Believe it or not, as you wish, but no one at school ever wanted to know what I knew."

It's quiet. I'm prepared to leave. A few days later, my bags already packed, Frau Lehnert calls me to her office again.

"You were right," she says. "I've looked at the work you did for all your classes. You were judged unfairly. I'm going to see to it personally that you're able to get your diploma."

I'm still mistrustful when I leave her office. Ten days later I'm instructed to report to Room 2-A for class.

IT'S THE LAST day nominations will be accepted for Head of the Student Body. The candidates are to be selected on the basis of overall excellence, fellowship and service.

A couple of my classmates come up to me and ask if I'm willing to have them nominate me. I turn around in disbelief to see if they're really talking to me. A couple of other students, who heard the first group ask me, put their heads together, whispering, and grin at me. I ignore them and to my own surprise say yes, almost so quiet it's inaudible.

It's winter. The day of the election, the first two periods are canceled. A thousand or so of us enter the Hall, where the elections will be held. When my name is called, I move clumsily across the hall to the podium. I see some faces that wish me well, others that are incredulous. I start out stuttering, then gradually become less nervous as I stand at the podium and give my short speech.

"First, I'd like to thank everyone who had the courage to nominate me for this position. I know there are many others in this room who are qualified for it, but we can only elect one person. I'm not first in my class—my grades aren't that great—but I can promise you I will always be there doing all I can wherever help and support are needed. I will advocate for anyone who can't make his or her needs known. With your support, I will devote myself to making sure that all students are treated fairly and with respect. I will demand that teachers take responsibility whenever favoritism or unfairness may arise. Of course, I hope that none of that will be necessary . . . "

71

I'm shaky as I leave the podium to loud applause, and suddenly it doesn't matter if I win the election. I've never before stood up in front of so many people—so many white people. Today I had the courage. After all the votes are cast and counted, I'm called back to the front of the hall.

"Erika has won an absolute majority. Please take the stand and state loudly and clearly whether you accept your elected office."

"I do."

After another year of school, I pass my exit exams solidly and must decide what sort of career to pursue. I'd still like to become a teacher, an elementary school teacher, but for that I would have to pass the *Abitur*, the exit exam of the academic high schools. I go to my teachers for advice.

"Some sort of career in social work would be best for you. To go back again and study for the *Abitur* at this point would be much too difficult for you. And we can't even be sure if you'd be taken on as a teacher. Why not spare yourself all that?"

I'm disappointed and uncertain, but I have faith in their advice and decide to begin the practical training course required to work in the field of child education and welfare. Two years later, I pass the licensing exam and apply for a job at a home in Frankfurt am Main. I'm ready to get out of the small-town environment and move to a city—a city so big that even I won't stand out.

I never expected to make the decision I did. Never planned to return to a children's home as a staff member. Considering my own experiences growing up in such a place, it is, perhaps, an astounding choice, but I don't really plan it. It just happens—I apply for the job because a former classmate did so a year a go. I have no parents or friends to advise me on this professional choice, and I am deeply ambivalent about it. I have no worse associations or memories than those from my time at the home where I grew up. I worry how I will cope, if the place I'm going turns out to be similar. My biggest challenge will be not to pass my own experiences unreflectively on to the children who will now be entrusted to my care. I'm certainly committed to doing everything differently from how it was done with me. I plan to deal differently with the concerns and needs of the children I work with, and I will always be alert to the unavoidable pitfalls of bringing them up in a racist society.

From the outside, the home where I will work looks just like all the other buildings on the street. But what will it be like inside? They're expecting me. A small, pale, slim woman, barely five foot three, opens the door. It's musty inside. The windows are all closed and I'm hot.

"Can I offer you a whiskey?" she asks when we're inside.

"Sure, I suppose I'd have a small glass," I say, to be polite.

Smiling and self-confident, the director of the home leaves the room and returns not with whiskey but a large cup of coffee, which she places before me.

"How long have you lived in Germany?" she asks, using *du*, the informal word for *you*. I have had this question asked of me so often, and it always stirs the same feelings, prods the same old wounds—for to me it carries the implication that I do not belong here, I'm not one of them, I don't have the same rights, I'm locked out. She continues: "Well, I hadn't realized you were . . . But it doesn't matter. We'll give you a try."

I know that I'll be greeted this way wherever I apply for work. I'm just happy to get the job. After the trial period is over, the director calls me to her office.

"If you continue to do your work as well as you've done it so far, we'll be only too pleased to have you stay on," she says. "Are you in agreement? Would you like to stay?"

I don't answer her directly, though I've made up my mind. I say: "I have one request, if I'm to stay. I'd like you to address me with the same formality you use with everyone else here. I'd like you to call me *Sie*, not *du*."

She says nothing. I leave her office.

I overhear my colleagues talking about me, sometimes quietly, sometimes not so. *Where do you think she's from? Not around here, that's clear enough—must have been a Negro involved. But what about the fact that she's allowed to work with children? I don't know. I suppose she'll be all right, if she has plenty of guidance and oversight.*

We're assigned in pairs to work with groups of children. My partner is small and wiry, with great, bulging eyes. Whenever the director enters the room where our group meets, she turns all her attention to her, hanging on her every word and scrambling to carry out her every wish. She's a nervous, clumsy, hasty woman. When we go out for walks, she tugs at the children in such a way that I'm fairly sure she's trying to keep any of them from coming too close to me. Her efforts only serve to make her a comic figure, though, and her obsequiousness has her in a state of constant anxiety. The moment she opens her mouth, the children draw together and there is complete silence. They stand up straight and do precisely as she bids them. Half-naked, towels draped over their shoulders, they line up and are marched into the shower room like a herd of cattle. They are supervised while they bathe, for which activity exactly fifteen minutes are allotted. Every two months, a barber descends on the home and gives every child the same hair cut.

Memories of my experiences at God's Little Acre are awakened in me. The atmosphere of this place and the way the children are treated are dreadfully familiar. I've integrated myself into this community rather quickly, but I'm not comfortable here. There is no doubt in my mind that I work at a detention center, not a "home" for children.

The time has come for me to do something. I tell the kids to call me by my first name; I cut their hair myself, if they want me to, or take them out to a salon, where I pay for their cuts myself. I let them shower individually and without supervision. I respect their need for privacy. I also resolve to go back to school again for a higher degree in social work and early childhood education. I want to expand my knowledge and test my practical experience against theory. I want some time to reflect. I request that my position be converted to half-time so I can attend classes. I'm granted permission and even told that I'll receive a fellowship for the last semester of the program so I can work full-time on completing the degree.

I enter the seminar room promptly at 8:00 A.M., and my first semester at the College of Social Work and

Pedagogy begins. The first thing I learn is to address the professors informally, as *du*. I discover that my previous insistence on respectful formality goes completely against the prevailing liberal norms. But I had never been exposed to such a world and had no way of knowing its norms. For me, using *Sie* has had very different implications than it has for the students and professors at the college: it was a positive thing, a sign of the respect that I craved, since everyone always assumed they could be informal with me, even when they used the formal *Sie* with my peers. This showed me they had no esteem for me and didn't consider me an equal.

I also learn to tolerate political groups of every sort, to distinguish right wing from left. I find out which professors give the best grades and which take attendance at lectures. I devote a great deal of time to reconciling all this new information with my past life experiences. I want to put what I'm learning to practical use, but are these theories really consistent with practice? I meet with other students in work groups, where we discus texts and test theses. It is not easy for me. I've never had the experience of being asked my opinion nor the privilege of inquiring into others' thought processes without being punished for it. The first few weeks I'm shy and tentative. I'm not confident enough to speak my mind. But with time I grow less inhibited and partake fervently in the discussions. Before long, my political consciousness has been raised, and it now demands that I become politically engaged in this country of mine. After two years, I graduate with high marks and am certified as a pedagogical social worker.

With my new degree in hand, I resume working full time at the home. But I've changed since I went back to

76

school. Now I work with all my might to make sure things are done the way I think they should be. I criticize the prevailing pedagogical methods and rebel against them. I refuse to follow or enforce rules set by the director unless they have some rational pedagogical basis. Before long, some of my co-workers have joined forces with me. I am able to convince them of my ideas and get them to follow my suggestions. We're in constant dialogue over how to run the home and evolve our own pedagogical model. Eventually, over the objections of certain colleagues and especially the director, we manage to implement a new model. Soon after, I am transferred to the personnel department of the home and threatened with termination on the grounds that "Miss Hügel is unreliable and immoral. She has no sense of the difference between doing her work and enjoying herself and has done permanent harm to the work of the home. People such as she should not be permitted to work with children." But I am not deterred from doing what I know is right and important.

In nine years, we transform what was effectively an overcrowded detention center into a place that is a real home to its residents. Instead of sixty-five children and youths, there are twenty, organized into several small groups that function as families. After twelve years at the home I resign, exhausted but deeply satisfied.

Even today, I maintain contact with children who grew up at the home. Some of them have their own families now and invite me to visit from time to time. I look back on my work at the home with pride. I undertook it as a mission, devoted myself to it absolutely and carried it through to completion.

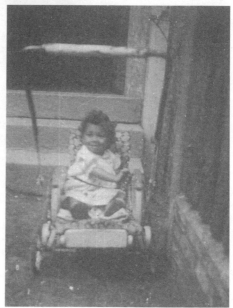

Eighteen months old.

With my mother.

With my grandmother, mother, and sister.

In the yard, in front of the barn.

A "visit" home.

(Right) God's Little
Acre Children's Home.

(Left) God's Little Acre
Children's Home, 1960.

The election for Head of Student Body in the town of Siegen, shortly before graduation from intermediate school.

With Dagmar Schultz in Berlin, 1995.

Three sisters in Berlin, 1997. (photo by Dagmar Schultz)

First meeting with my father, Chicago, 1993. (photo by Dagmar Schultz)

IT'S COLD AND stormy out. The wind beats rain into my face, and there's water in my shoes when I arrive at my usual café. This is where I come to drink coffee, read the paper and relax after seminars. My regular place—a small round table off in one corner—is still free. My shoes squeak on the floor as I hurry over and sit down, cold and tired. While I'm waiting to order, I notice a man just as wet as I am sitting right across from me. His hair is soaked through and hangs dripping in his face. He rifles rather desperately through his briefcase and his coat pockets, and I have to suppress a smile at his awkwardness. I stand up and offer him a handkerchief.

"Oh, how did you know . . ."

"I got soaked too and couldn't help noticing that you were searching for something to wipe your face with."

"Thanks. I'm Alexander."

"Ika."

"Would you like to join me?"

"Sure. Why not? Let me grab my things."

I feel awkward when I first sit down with him, but we don't leave the café until night has fallen.

Alexander lives outside the city, but we meet again at the café and spend many hours talking about politics, travel, and my studies. We're evaluating each other. Then one day it dawns on me: I'm falling in love with his cautious, sometimes awkward ways. Or maybe it's his hapless attempts to express his affection, or the growing openness between us. But whatever it is, I find I'm ready to make a commitment. After half a year together, we decide to marry.

"You, get married? You'll never be anything more than a plaything for men."

"But do you really want to get married? Think of the children. They'll have just as hard a time as you did, and you of all people know what it's like not to belong. Honestly, I want every happiness for you, but people will talk. And no matter how strong your relationship is, how can it survive that? You'll find out, but I'm afraid I'm only too right about that."

Alex and I are sitting on a narrow bench in a long hall. We've been here a half an hour, waiting to register for our marriage. I look at him: He is tall and thin, he has blue green eyes and dark brown, slightly curly hair. He's dressed casually but stylishly. He smiles at me. I lose myself in my thoughts and am startled when a door opens and a gaunt, pale, rather unattractive middle-aged man emerges and extends his hand.

"Good afternoon."

Alex and I stand up to return his greeting, but the man turns his back to me and takes Alex's hand. He asks loudly: "But what's this, haven't you brought your bride-to-be along with you? She must be here too, you know, if we're to proceed."

I sit back down. We look at one another. Then Alex takes my arm and explains to this bureaucrat that I am his bride. For a moment, I'm shocked. Then I want to scream, maybe from the pain this encounter causes me but also from sheer wrath it stirs up. I feel powerless. I try to tell myself that this is nothing new, just the logical extension of everything I have already experienced in my life. Alex and I never talk about it. Four weeks later, we're married in a civil ceremony, and afterward, as we descend the grand steps of the courthouse, a man dressed in the formal attire of another wedding party steps forward and respectfully congratulates my maid of honor on her marriage.

I am troubled by this continual need to point out to others that it is I who am getting married, but on the other hand I don't want to let it spoil my day, so I push all those feelings to the side and celebrate. My family is happy that I'm in good hands—none of them ever thought I'd marry either. Alexander's parents, who have been divorced for some years, are both there with us as well.

Alexander loves to cook and splits the housework with me. Weekends, he brings me breakfast in bed. We travel a good deal, and through him I learn about other cultures and people. There are times, when we're away, that I wish we would never return to Germany. I never learned to love my country and understand little about it—except that I know I'm not wanted there.

Two years is not a long time, but we settle into certain routines and patterns of behavior. We've stopped talking to each other with the openness and honesty we once did. I am forced to acknowledge that my marriage won't protect me from discrimination or the jeers of passersby. *Look at that one—thinks she someone, just because she's got a white man on her arm. Oh, look—it won't last long between those two. Couldn't she find one of her own kind to pair off with? Did it absolutely have to be a German man?*

I become increasingly aware that my relationship with Alexander has changed, and I pelt him with questions: *Why don't we do things together anymore, the way we used to? Are you ashamed of me? Why won't you let me take your arm in public anymore?* He dodges every time. *No one looks at you any differently than they do me. You're imagining it. You're just being paranoid. You're my wife, aren't you? What makes you think things are any different between other married couples? You're brown skinned—so what? I married you, didn't I? You ought to know by now I've never gone in for that touchy-feely stuff.*

Three years have passed, and I feel increasingly alone and dissatisfied. My husband is ever more reluctant to let himself be seen with me. He is testy, nervous, and often goes out without me. When we meet new people, I detect their incomprehension and disbelief, and even a bit of scorn, at the fact that we're a couple—much less a married couple. *What? I thought she was just a friend of yours. That's your wife? You got yourself an ethnic one, eh? She doesn't look half bad to me.*

Alexander does everything possible to avoid public displays of intimacy. He does not hold my hand. It's been ages since he put his arm around my waist. In the subway and on streetcars, he sits some distance away from me. I keep coming back to the idea it must be me, something I've done. I'm too awkward or I just don't behave the way a black wife should toward her white husband. I imagine that other women act more naturally than I do when they're at home with their husbands. I live in constant fear of displeasing him. Increasingly I notice how ashamed he is of me and how difficult it is for him to take the remarks that other people make about me, or us. He goes out on his own a lot, now, and is less and less interested in what I'm doing and thinking. I'm in a constant state of fear and uncertainty. Many days we start arguing as soon as we get up in the morning.

92

"Children? You want children? With me? I don't—not with you."

I say nothing. Inside I'm raging, hurting, confused. I carry the pain around with me for a long time, knowing that this isn't even the worst of my torments. The worst is that Alexander can't even talk to me about his fears, his helplessness. Every time I try to open up with him, to make him better understand my experience of racism, he puts me off, makes me feel guilty. *I can't even talk to you, you're so sensitive. You take offense at everything.* He cannot imagine us fighting discrimination together and thereby fighting against the gradual destruction of our marriage. He doesn't know how.

Alexander walks out. He falls in love with another woman. I meet her. I go to her apartment and pace back and forth in front of the building. Finally, carefully, I knock.

"Come in." She is tall and thin. Her pale face is framed by a brightly printed headband, and she's wearing a woolen shawl over her shoulders. She puts out her hand and invites me inside. We talk about nothing, and I wonder what I'm doing there. I don't really want to know her or how she differs from me. We stop talking, look at each other silently for a few moments, and then I get up and leave without another word.

It's not easy for me to grasp that Alexander and I have no future together, but I'm able to let him go. I can't stand jealousy. I do feel it, deep within me, but competing against whites is dangerous. I let him go. For a short time I thought my marriage to this white man had finally made me a full-fledged member of the society I live in, respected, perhaps, even admired. I was wrong.

I've learned my lesson: Whites just can't confront the issues of racism. They dare not question their own values, because for them, putting things in question would mean questioning their own privilege. Who does such a thing willingly? Who can bear to? It's not about the fact that all whites are racists; the point is how they deal with that fact.

How could I have expressed my rage? How might I have protected myself from being hurt by his racism, so that I wouldn't have had to question him, my husband, or my marriage?

I am always coming up against this choice: Either I swallow my rage and let it devour me from within or I take the liberty of articulating it, forge a new basis for self-respect and free myself from being defined as "foreign."

Alexander and I divorce after six years.

"You've created the conflicts, and now you want me to be the one who goes through with the divorce, not you."

I was just attempting to discuss our problems, but this so threatens Alexander that he's taken it for a suggestion that we divorce. The questions I asked him are no different than those I've asked him many times before. The difference is that now I'm better able to deal with the consequences of his response.

"Do you want to be free of me, then? Do you want to give up the past and all that we've been to each other? If that's what you want, I accept it, and I'll try to understand."

But how can I ever be free of the past, when my present reality repeats it?

"You say I never asked you what it was like to grow up black in a racist society. Why should I have to ask you? Don't you think you conveyed it to me constantly, every single day? What more could you have told me? I knew it all. Isn't the important thing that I dealt with it?"

So many people go about their lives believing in good conscience that they're capable of acting on others' behalf, when really they've never even stopped to ask what those other people want. Seeing something isn't the same as understanding it. Not asking is the same thing as not wanting to know. And someone who asks no questions is, in the final analysis, not ready to question his own ways of thinking and acting.

"It's clear to me that you've got a new identity, a new sense of who you are, and that there's no place there for me. I'm glad you've made new friends, and I hope they'll see you through."

The changes in me seem to trigger panic in white people. The poor, pitiful creature they knew is no longer behaving as they expect. I'm throwing them for a loop. And what could be more fitting or appropriate than to dish me up a small reminder of my helplessness, just to make sure I know they're the only ones who can offer me honesty, friendship, or love?

I ought to have learned by now that change means loss. I ought to be more careful with the few whites who have been genuine with me, shown me love— even if it means I must be silent and unquestioningly accept their love and honesty. I really ought not to go changing myself without their approval. I ought to have realized that even my women friends would just get defensive and shirk responsibility for their own behavior, as soon as I started to ask tough questions or to change.

White people can't expect me to give them the benefit of the doubt. It's a sign of intimacy, friendship, respect, when I gradually do establish such trust.

Survival in a racist society is something whites take for granted. They don't even notice that racism exists. They think that they alone hold the power in this culture to lift the likes of me up from the sewers, and that they can drop me back down there whenever they please. But no, they've been thinking too much about their own hands. In reality, they can only do away with someone who's still in their clutches. When will the many oh-so-helpful whites wake up and realize they never held a human being in their hands? At most, they had me by the shirt collar.

"As you above all people know, we live in a society where there's racism—overt as well as covert. But you should also realize that that doesn't mean *society itself* is racist. Broad generalizations like that lead straight to disaster, so please, just don't go there."

Well, what should I call a society where the racism is overt as well as covert, if not *racist*? But just how whites want to describe their society is irrelevant to me. It is I, not they, who have had to struggle with the disastrous results wrought by that society, every day of my life.

"THE PERSONAL IS political." This motto comes from the women's movement—the white women's movement—but I adopt it as my own.

My friends Carola, Ursula, and I decide to move into a communal apartment. They bring their own furniture and most of what we'll need to outfit the kitchen. I go out twice a week on trash days and scavenge what I need for my own room. It takes me weeks to strip, refinish, and fix it all up. It's the first time I've had a room I decorated myself, and I'm proud of it.

Everywhere now, there are women's bars, women's cafés, and all-women communal apartments springing up. One evening when we're sitting around the kitchen table, we decide to start a women's shelter. It doesn't take us long to find a little house in the courtyard behind a commercial building in a fairly central location. It's the first women's shelter in Frankfurt. There's a library on the top floor with separate reading and rec rooms. We turn the ground floor into a bar, but when we're all off at a demonstration, it stays closed for the day.

There are plenty of reasons to demonstrate. Every weekend, Carola, Ursula, and I set out for some protest or political gathering or other. Thousands of women move through the streets. We speak out, make ourselves heard and, as we march, we bring women we see standing uncertainly by the wayside into the fold. Our biggest and most successful event is a pro-choice march from the Frankfurt Women's Center to Holland under a banner reading DOWN WITH § 218, the legal paragraph that contains the language outlawing abortion. Every waystation is a chance to increase our numbers, and the collective voice of the marchers grows louder in every town we pass through. We make our demands known on printed balloons and banners. We arrange for women in need to travel to Holland for abortions. Frequently, I go with them as an escort and advisor. Singly and in groups, we are fighting for equal rights and against oppression.

But not against racism. None of my sisters in the women's groups—no one in the entire women's movement, in fact—is interested in hearing the story of black women's struggles. They don't want to see that our society is racist as well as sexist. These white feminists don't understand that they too are the beneficiaries of the racist status quo or that the pervasiveness of racism allows them to ignore that black and white skin are not accorded equal value. The more my political consciousness grows within this context and the more the women's movement influences my thinking, the slower comes my dawning awareness of how prevalent racism is. It will not be until much later, when I become involved with the black and Afro-German movements, that the connections between racist and sexist oppression are fully clear to me.

One Sunday I'm sitting in the center of the room during a big meeting at the Women's Center. I stand up and make my way to the window, where I can better see and hear the other women. I'm hot, and I don't know how long I stand there bathed in sweat before I finally summon the courage to say what's on my mind: "As a black woman, I feel that our struggle for equality against sexism and oppression has overlooked the problem of racism." All eyes are on me, and in them I

98

can see reluctance, annoyance, a lack of understanding. For this one moment, I wish I hadn't spoken. Fear surges up in me, and I'm not sure I'm up to the discussion that will inevitably ensue from my statement. I would prefer to leave the room and avoid hearing their aggressive statements, get out of having to make all the old familiar arguments. But I don't. I stay.

Words, sympathy, communal laughter. And I'm feeling it again: pain that strikes me to the core. I don't let it show. I don't come out and tell them how I feel. I'm not going to call them on their racism just yet. I'll wait a while. I've learned it's not worth jeopardizing my connection to these people for a single moment. They're not ready to hear it yet. I need to give them time, give them a chance. I'm just glad that this is something they're willing to discuss with me.

"Come on, you know we're different from other women. How could we, as feminists, have anything against blacks? If you have a specific problem to raise, okay, but try to leave skin color out of it."

I feel faceless. They make me feel I have no right to feel.

"Being white, we can't judge whether you perceive us as racist. If you think about it that way, it's actually you who determines what is and isn't racism."

And thus they cast themselves as my victims, wronged by my harsh judgment. I'm the one holding the reins while all these white feminists tremble before me.

"So what are you saying? We're just racists, regardless of all our idealism? We're no better than the typical white person after all?"

So I'm supposed to be grateful that any white people at all would stand up for me or my interests—if that's what they're doing. And if I want more than just words—if I want words backed up by actions—that makes me ungrateful.

"As a feminist, I must tell you that while there are some situations in which it's important to confront racism, this isn't one of them. And speaking as a white woman and feminist, I'd like to suggest to you that every white person's socialization process is unique. People's life stories can go a long way toward explaining their attitudes and needs—which may have very little to do with racism after all. Of course, I can't argue with the fact that you perceive such people as racist, but couldn't that really be just a perception you have because of your own life story as a black woman?"

I really ought to restrict my accusations of racism to those outside our movement; I shouldn't strike out at those who are close to me. My perceptions may generally be correct, but clearly there are also situations in which they are inaccurate.

It's a first step, this theoretical engagement with the problem of racism, but it's all too easy for whites to hide from the actual, unbearable situation that I and other black women find ourselves in. All they have to do is refuse to hear us or hear us only half way.

Clever words can mask a great deal, but trust is created only when strong words are meant seriously and backed up by actions. It doesn't matter how I describe my injuries or couch my reproaches, no one ever says, "I'm sorry." This is where my first real conflict with them arises.

"We're not here just to deal with your personal problems. You're so self-absorbed, interested in us only when it serves your own purposes. And you're turning everything around so it's about you. Do you even understand the problems we're coping with here?"

Here I am, a black woman, shamelessly exploiting her white sisters and ignoring their problems. They don't want me to get too used to having a big deal made over the issue of racism, and so, no matter how passionately I feel about my experiences, no matter how real and profound my sense of exclusion may be, they would be grateful if I could please refrain from disparaging whites just to make my point.

Every interaction I have with whites comes down to this. I have to be on my guard. I have to protect myself. But how long am I going to continue to accept their shocked attitudes and false consciousness? How long will I continue to bear the brunt of their anger? How much longer can I continue to minimize the effects of their attitude toward me or to come up with justifications for it? How much longer will I buy that they're just asking for my consideration, when actually they are being cowards? How long?

My skin color doesn't change, but with each year that passes, I grow older, stronger and smarter—living alongside white people, I have no other choice—but I don't want to grow complacent. I know that some whites are at least theoretically committed to fighting against injustice, but it is I who am impacted by that injustice. It's not easy for me to be candid with whites or to enter into frank discussions with them. I'm constantly wary of being insulted and hyper-alert to any signs of discrimination. It takes enormous effort to maintain sincerity and distrust simultaneously, and it throws me into a state of permanent anxiety.

101

Every now and then I wonder what it would be like to meet other black people, to listen to them talk, to hear what they say, to know what it would feel like to be among blacks.

I think about my father more and more often. The intense need to have a father is with me always, but I reject it. I forbid myself to feel this desire. I am so frightened and shut down that I can't even imagine meeting my father. The idea that I might somehow, discover him myself is inconceivable.

Blacks are utterly strange to me, and I fear them. I've come to hold certain beliefs about them by generalizing from my own case: I am black and I am ugly, awful to look at with hair so wild no stylist could tame it. I'm a bad seed, wayward, immoral, filthy, stupid. The last person I'd want to meet is someone like me.

My new apartment is tiny—it doesn't even compare to the place I had with my ex—but I feel at home here because it is mine and mine alone. Even so, sometimes when I get home I just sit in front of the television, trying to pass the time until I go to bed. I have only a few pieces of furniture and a rocking horse Alexander gave me when we were together. I take possession of the space slowly, putting my books in the shelves and my paint brushes and drawing pads in their newly assigned places. The room I spend the least time in is the kitchen. I never learned to enjoy cooking. Now and then I make myself a pot of coffee or cook up yet another plate of spaghetti, but mostly I eat at friends' houses or get take-out.

I must change something about my life, I think, and for the first time in ages I hang up my coat on the rack instead of tossing it over the back of a chair. I pick up the newspaper and plop down on the couch, even though I'm too tired to read. I flip the pages distractedly and my eyes land on a bold printed advertisement: TAE KWON DO FOR WOMEN, MONDAYS AND WEDNESDAYS, 7–9:00 P.M.

It's just what I need right now: a martial arts class, working out, meeting new people. Within the week I have begun training with five other new women.

Sunny is more than just my Tae Kwon Do instructor. From the first instant, she makes me feel welcome. I can hardly believe any white person, but especially one I've just met, could offer me so much consideration and respect. Until now, I've always had to prove myself to people. With Sunny, I don't feel the need to prove that I'm just as good, just as capable, just as weak or strong, or just as likable as my white sisters. She demands the utmost from me in class. She pushes me to train harder and overcome my self-imposed limits, to open myself to new energy, not to give up, to focus, to believe in myself and my abilities.

There are twenty-five women in training at the school, and the atmosphere is one of friendly open-mindedness. I am the only black woman, but I encounter no racism, neither tacit nor overt. I don't know what the other women think of me or whether they know other blacks. The entire tone of the place is set by Sunny's personality and her insistence that there is no place for racism, sexism, or discrimination of any sort in Tae Kwon Do training. All the women treat one another—and even me—with tolerance and respect. The school is an entirely positive place for me. I'm learning the art of Tae Kwon Do. Remarkably, I'm doing it in an environment where racism is not inherent.

I am overjoyed to be in training at this school and to have Sunny as a teacher, even if I sometimes rebel against the training, grow angry, and feel that Sunny is too harsh. She knows my limits better than I do. Every class, she extracts a little more will power or persistence from me. She teaches me that self-knowledge—my own awareness of my strengths, the language of my own body, and how I hold myself—is far more important than any other quality anyone has ever attributed to me. Every day, Tae Kwon Do changes my life. I learn not only to take myself seriously as an opponent, a combatant, but to demand respect while fighting. These are lessons I will carry with me throughout the rest of my life.

In time, Sunny and I also become close friends. One night, after class, she hands me a newspaper clipping, an article about the first-ever national gathering of Afro-Germans, which will be taking place in the near future, right here in Frankfurt. *Afro-Germans*? What kind of word is that? I tell myself I'm not interested and toss the paper in the trash can. Why would I want anything to do with "people of my own kind"? There's no way I'm going to that meeting. I'm not prepared to give up my anonymity. Why should I make myself visible all of a sudden, for whom? I don't want to look into "Afro-German" faces and see more of my own pain. I'm far too afraid of reliving all I've worked so hard to put behind me, and my hatred of the color of my skin far outweighs any desire I might have to meet other Afro-German men and women.

I'm used to this life, to being excluded, to being different, to being angry, to the fact that my very existence is considered improper by the majority of Germans. My own understanding of injustice has thus far sufficed to ensure my survival. I'm not ready—not yet—to join a community of people like myself. I don't want to hear what they have to say and I don't want to deal with their pain, which is all too likely the same pain I have experienced.

I'm used to being in conflict with whites, and therefore I find that state of conflict less threatening than the possibility that I might come into conflict with other blacks. I know whites will never change, but at least this provides me with a certain security—I know what to expect.

Then, about six months later, I receive a completely unexpected phone call from an Afro-German woman who invites me in a friendly, warm voice to another gathering of Afro-Germans. I decide on the basis of her call that I'll do it—I'll go and meet these Afro-Germans.

I'm getting my things together, getting ready to leave the apartment just as I would any other day, having finished my coffee before going to a meeting, to Tae Kwon Do, to a party, to a reading. But today I'm a little nervous—I'm on my way to meet the Afro-German group. I don't trust myself. I'm not sure that I really want to take up all the issues of racism and being black or to enter into dialogue about them with other blacks.

I leave the house and don't let myself stop moving the whole way there, lest I lose my momentum and turn back around. Twenty minutes later, I walk into an apartment where there are already twelve other Afro-Germans. They welcome me warmly.

"We're so glad you came."

One woman even tells me: "I'm so glad you exist." And then, "Come on, let's sit down and eat. We all want to hear how things are going for everyone."

I am speechless.

A Dream Is Over

Scraps of dreams and daydreams rise
up in my body.
Dreamdances.
As if there were a light brightening the space around
me.
I am not black, not white,
I am permeable, transparent.
It startles me when I realize everyone can see me.
Exhausted, I lean back against a wall
and let my body collapse.
I'm glowing—and through this sensation of welcome
and
arrival, I look into faces that mirror my own.
I close my eyes and consider the eternity
that lies between my longing and my loneliness. I am
tempted and want to go toward them,
just a bit closer.
My fear creeps up over my shoulders,
and I look at my brown hands.
I want to call out,
"I need hands, your brown hands."
But the merest touch would cause my body
to shatter.
My breathing grows quiet.

We meet every week, talk on the phone, take care of each other. I am moved by the experience and at first I don't really understand what is happening to me. I leave each meeting intoxicated, and it takes half the week for me to come back down to Earth. I don't know what's more unbelievable—the thirty-nine years in which I lived in total isolation, never seeing a black face that wasn't my own, or the fact that now, suddenly, I'm not alone any more. I now see that I have always compared myself to whites and have almost uniformly judged them to be better, superior in every pursuit, worthier of respect, preferable. After all, they hadn't questioned themselves every day of their lives. Now that I've met other Afro-Germans, I see for the first time that differences can unite people, not just divide them. We acknowledge each others' strengths and weaknesses, and not just as a collective—each and every one of us does it him or herself, in his or her own way. The color of our skin and our common struggle to survive create a bond between us that we have never felt among whites.

I'm not all by myself at the edge of this world anymore. I belong to a group that wants me to belong. Our meetings are characterized by mutual respect and attentiveness. Survival is no longer a question of strength or pride; it is a decision.

This new sense of having a community has empowered me and strengthened my personality. The changes in me don't go unnoticed by my white friends. *So, are you reading a lot of black literature these days? I've heard that's the newest thing. And what do you know about all that cultural criticism—can you make heads or tails of it? Maybe you could give me a few pointers.*

Oh, but you're not really very black, exactly. I've known you so long I don't even see it anymore. You could actually pass as an Italian, you know.

Just be glad you weren't born with a handicap and that you were able to learn a profession. There are plenty of people in the world worse off.

What do you think you're going to do now, go to America just because there are more blacks over there? Well, all the blacks in America are criminals. And you say your father's there, but do you really know that? What do you want with him anyway? It's pretty obvious he doesn't want anything to do with you.

You know, if you didn't make such a big deal about it, no one would even know you were mixed—sorry about the expression, but there it is.

Step by step, I begin to discover who I am. In the meetings with my brothers and sisters, I am set free from the self-doubt and pain—some of which is on the surface, some of which has long been buried—that whites created in me and ultimately trained me to feel, all the while accusing me of hypersensitivity. I am able to believe in myself, to take myself seriously and to unlearn much of what whites have taught me. I even begin to love myself, my skin color, everything that I am—but slowly, carefully. Every time I repossess a part of my heart or my body, it hurts. And finally, I discover that I can love myself as well as my brothers and sisters.

With my newly won self-assurance there also comes a sense of indignation and outrage. I am enraged with all those who have shirked responsibility for what I've endured, with all those who did not want me to survive. I should not have to strive to be acknowledged or wanted. Never again will I stand politely by while people look down on me. I will no longer trust the type of person who, having just hurt me with their words or attitudes, then bursts into tears because they can't take my pain or my anger at them. They caused that anger. I'm no longer troubled by the possibility that whites will distance themselves from me if I don't behave in a manner they expect. I've struggled long enough without any support from those people, and I survived it, but I'm not going to fight against myself anymore.

As long as I don't know what I want, others will decide for me. As long as I don't define myself, others will. As long as I don't know who I am, others will try to tell me who I ought to be. My mother thought *Erika* was a beautiful name, the most beautiful name she could give me, and till now I've always liked it. But I decide that from here on out I will call myself *Ika*. Almost everyone else does, too.

All across the country at this time, we Afro-Germans are beginning to make our histories visible, to take control of our lives. Have we ever heard anything about the history of blacks in this country? Have we ever heard of the first black student in Germany, who graduated from the University of Halle in 1729, having written his dissertation on the history of blacks in Europe? Have we ever heard that during the Nazi period, blacks, too, were persecuted, sterilized, deported and murdered in the concentration camps?

In every large city, groups come together and form local chapters of the nationwide Black German Initiative (*Initiative Schwarze Deutsche* or ISD). We call ourselves *Afro-Germans* or *black Germans*, thus coining a new name for ourselves with which we can identify. Most of us have been labeled *mixed-race* or *Mulatto* all our lives. For others it was *occupation baby*, though the presence of a considerable black population in Germany predates and has nothing to do with World War II. Before long, we begin to publish a magazine for black women, *Afrekete*, and another for black Germans in general, *Afro-Look*. An Afro-German women's organization called ADEFRA is founded and initiates many groups in many German cities. When the book *Showing Our Colors: Afro-German Women in Search of Their History** is published, its impact continues to be felt through the time of Reunification in 1989, helping put Afro-German women from the former East Germany in touch with their history. A documentary film is made about the African woman Machbuba, who, one hundred fifty years ago, was brought to the town of Muskau, near Cottbus, by Prince Pückler. An international network of black German women springs up, stemming partly from a three-week-long conference held in Germany in 1991, called the Intercultural Summer Institute for Women's Studies. Beginning in 1985, the ISD organizes the annual celebration of Black History Month in Berlin. I attend conferences for black, immigrant, and Jewish women, where I learn that blacks are not in fact the smallest minority in Germany and that we need not remain isolated unto ourselves.

The more I learn about black history, the more I want to meet my father.

* *Farbe Bekennen; Afro-deutsche Frauen auf den Spuren ihrer Geschichte*—English title my translation.

"I'm sure he must be dead by now, and where would you start looking or him? America is enormous." My mother says this, or something like it, every time I mention my desire to find him. I hear uncertainty in her voice. It doesn't seem she has much to tell me about him.

She does remember how her friends always said I looked like him. *She's the spitting image. Cut from the same cloth.* I ask her to call around and see if any of her friends have old pictures with him in them, but when she asks, they don't want to be reminded of that time. They tell her coolly no, they have no such pictures. It's an attempt, at least. An attempt to use a picture to get a small bit closer to this man. I'm impressed by my mother's courage and determination in approaching her old friends, one after another, though each one rejects her in turn.

In 1990, I decide to move to Berlin, where I've been offered a job, and I'm optimistic that I will meet people there who'll be able to help me pursue my search for my father.

It's in Berlin that I come back into contact with the poet-activist Audre Lorde, whom I first met in 1987.

She was coming to Frankfurt for a conference, and a friend and I were assigned to pick her up from the airport. I was extremely excited to be meeting her—I'd read a great deal of her work and been greatly influenced by it. Her texts gave me courage and made me feel understood. I'd rediscovered myself, not only in the way she expressed the pain that I and so many blacks felt, but also in her message that we must stop seeing ourselves as helpless victims of a racist system. As we waited for her plane that day, I paced back and forth chain-smoking cigarettes, frustrated that precisely this

111

flight had to be delayed. Finally, with her life's partner, Gloria Joseph, and her German publisher, Dagmar Schultz, at her side, Audre Lorde walked through the cordoned-off arrival area and straight toward me. She put her arms around me and hugged me to her and said my name. I was stunned, not just by her heartfelt greeting and radiating warmth, the likes of which I'd never felt from any other person, but also that she knew my name. It turned out she'd seen pictures from the first Afro-German conference held in Munich. She had asked the name of each participant and remembered us all. I was delighted by her spontaneous warmth and felt an immediate connection to her. I'd never so quickly come to feel close to another person nor opened myself up as easily as I did with Audre Lorde.

Beginning in 1984, Audre spent several weeks in Berlin each year, usually with her partner, Gloria. She always gave as many readings as possible. Men and women of every sort turned out and were affected by her work. Sometimes there was resistance or controversy, but no one ever left one of her readings without having been strongly impacted. In particular, she urged us black women to raise our voices and demand equal rights and respect from the society we lived in.

Picking up Audre for the Frankfurt conference was also the first time I met Dagmar, and we developed a deep and intimate relationship. Her love and trust have enabled me to approach painful facts and experiences as well as passionate, beautiful things differently than ever before. We support one another, learn from one another, take one another's side and tell one another what has happened to us in our lives. We talk about what it was like to grow up in a racist society—she tells me what it was like for her as a white person; I tell her my experiences as a black person. We are united in struggle, particularly the struggle against everyday racism. We are there for each other. We share great and small sorrows, happiness, and joy. Our bond is a very close one. Dagmar is an irreplaceable part of my life.

In 1992 and 1993, Audre spends several months staying with Dagmar and me at our Berlin apartment. During that time, Audre never passes up an opportunity to discuss issues of racism and difference between women. It is the first time anyone has so fully and frequently engaged me on these issues, and Audre's words have stayed with me ever since, influenced the course of my political engagement. She is a magnetic person on her own, and her interest in me bonds me to her all the more.

"Always remember how proud I am of you and all black Germans. Everything that you are, Ika, and everything you amount to, you have achieved for yourself. Your will to survive and your fight against injustice and racism have made you strong." Audre encourages me and insists that I end my silence. She urges me not to let my fears deter me from speaking out. And since that time, I have undertaken to express myself unreservedly and to make my opinion known, whenever I am in a discussion or dispute with a white German.

"I'm fed up with your well meaning, superficial understanding. I want nothing to do with your shock, your tears of self-pity, or your complicity. I don't want your contrition unless you're also able to take responsibility for the consequences of your actions. You always find some excuse for what you've done. Well, I'm no longer available as a test case for you to practice becoming enlightened on."

113

IT FINALLY HAPPENS in 1990, after nine years of Tae Kwon Do training: I go to America.

Four other women and I are on our way from Germany to Columbus, Ohio, where we will take part in a week-long training camp, at the end of which I will compete for my black belt. I am so nervous I feel my heart may burst as the plane approaches New York City. This is my father's country. Does that make it mine? My whole body trembles—it's as if I were actually about to meet him. How in the world will I manage to get off this airplane in one piece? As I disembark, this anxiety and an overwhelming feeling of longing for my father overtake me. Everything seems out of kilter, even those things that were more or less in order just moments before. In the airport, every mature black man I see is my father. I barely speak English but I want to run up and start talking to any or all of them. I'm too shy to actually do it. I could just walk up to them, stand before them and say nothing, but what kind of person would do that? Then, before we've gotten far into the airport, several black people nod and smile or say hello to me. I don't know how to respond. Where I come from, only people who are already acquainted greet each other in public. This friendliness, this phenomenon of being seen and acknowledged by people I don't even know, this tacit connection to other blacks all touch me in precisely the place where my longing for membership in a group and deliverance from isolation reside. I am dazed, but I return their greetings, hoping that this will go on and on, all day long.

"Do you know them?" asks my training partner.

"No," I say, rather proudly. "But I know why they're greeting me."

She shakes her head, probably thinking I've gone crazy.

That night, exhausted and hungry from the flight, we go out to a pizzeria, but the very first bite turns my stomach. I'm unable to eat a thing and go outside to get some air. I burst unexpectedly into tears. I have no words to explain why I'm crying, but as if from a great distance, I feel my yearning for my father. I look at my feet in disbelief that they are truly standing on the ground of my father-land. My sobs come faster and I'm not sure how I'll explain what I'm feeling to the others—I don't understand it myself. Somewhere, somehow, maybe I'll meet him, I think, but there isn't much time. Then I go back inside and apologize to everyone for having left the table so abruptly.

As we've planned, Dagmar arrives at the end of the strenuous week of training and she's there to see me receive my first *Dan* , or title of mastery, after I pass the tests to become a black belt. I'm ecstatic as I take my black belt from the hand of the master. I look into Sunny's and Dagmar's eyes and see that these two alone in the room understand just how much this means to me. It's about far more than winning a black belt. They are proud of me. We're planning to go from here to the Caribbean to visit Audre and Gloria on St. Croix. I pack my black belt in my suitcase.

It's high summer, and the air is so humid I can barely breathe when we land in St. Croix. I've been looking forward to this trip for a long time. Gloria and Audre are there to meet us at the gate with a bottle of

Champagne to celebrate my earning the black belt. It takes forever for our suitcases to appear on the baggage carousel, and while we wait, I look around with curiosity. Everywhere there are black people. For the first time, I'm counting how many whites there are in a roomful of blacks. I'm happy, though exhausted by the trip and the climate. On our way to their house, "Judith's Fancy," I have a feeling of timelessness, as if there were no beginning or end, a feeling of well being and centeredness. The royal poinciana are covered with blood red flowers, and it smells like sun and sea. At the house, Gloria's dog, Beaver, greets us enthusiastically, as if he knew us. It's around one o'clock, and we have the whole afternoon ahead of us. Gradually, despite my excitement and curiosity, tranquility steals over me. St. Croix is sun, quiet, warmth. I have the exhilarating idea that I could be at home here, I could belong—quite naturally. Before long, I begin to feel a certain ownership of this place, different from how I've felt about any other place I've ever been, and I know that no one can ever dispossess me of it.

Audre and Gloria have invited us to join them at a performance in town later in the day, and I look forward to it with near impatience. Children large and small perform skits and do dances to thunderous applause. For the second time, I count people the opposite way from what I'm used to: there are three whites among hundreds of blacks. I cannot even imagine what it might have been like to grow up being praised, celebrated, applauded, marveled at, taught, supported, and loved by other black people. Audre puts her arm around me—she seems to sense and understand what I'm feeling. I feel I have arrived. My time here—all the moments, impressions, pictures, and encounters with black people—will have an enormous impact on me for the rest of my life. I know now that in the long term, I would be happier among black people—freer, more full of life. After this trip, these wonderful weeks, I will return to St. Croix for my vacation every year. It becomes my annual homecoming.

In October 1992, Dagmar and I are invited to lecture at Amherst College. Audre flies to New York with us, having just spent the past three months in Berlin, where she completed a three-month course of cancer treatment. Audre will be staying in New York to see specialists before flying back home to St. Croix. Dagmar and I press on toward Amherst. Half an hour before our train departs, we pull up in a cab at West 100th Street.

"Audre, we'll be there with you before your birthday in February."

"I'll try to be there, too," she says and we hug each other with more affection than ever, now that we all know her time is limited. She is tired, very tired, and very sick. Three months, I think, are an infinity to one who's looking into death's eyes. "Whenever you need us, we'll be there, we'll come," I tell her. It's October, and my heart is full of sorrow. The pain of this leave-taking wraps around my chest like a band. My breathing comes heavy. Soon Audre will be gone forever, never to return, and I can't go with her. All I can do is stay by her side and try to bring some comfort to her last hours.

They're expecting us at Amherst. We arrive only an hour before my lecture is to begin. My talk will address race crimes and race-related violence in Germany, which have been on the the increase since the fall of the Berlin Wall in 1989, and what might be done to stop them. Every seat in the house is full.

118

"You'll do a great job up there. I'm proud of you," Audre whispered to me, just before we left. Her words echo in my head as I give my speech.

". . . Acts of racially motivated violence take place every day. There are still places in my country where blacks cannot use public transportation. Many fear to go out in the street after dark. Mothers stop taking their children to kindergarten because of racist attacks. On the street, blacks are beaten up in broad daylight— consider the case of Angolan immigrant Antonio Amide, who died of injuries sustained in a racially motivated assault. A group of skinheads used a pair of scissors to cut off part of the tongue of a Polish man. Jewish graveyards and monuments are desecrated, the most recent instance being a barracks in the former concentration camp of Sachsenhausen, which has been made into a Holocaust memorial museum.

"Every day refugee shelters are stoned or set on fire with Molotov cocktails. Two Afro-German women on their way home after a vacation were subjected to body-cavity searches in a German airport. One of the officials explained to them that, "Race is now one of our selection criteria." This racial violence exists through-out Germany, but it's worst in the former East German states. A great number of black Germans have decided, for all these reasons, to leave Germany—their home-land. It was not an easy decision for many of them, and has also been painful for those who remain behind.

"Well, the Afro-German community is no longer willing to endure conditions that force them out of their country. We are part of the German population— we've been there a long time—and now we are fight-ing for a place within our own society. We are fighting for the place that is rightfully ours.

119

"Despite the racist attacks, we will continue to fight. We will not give up. It is up to us to create a history for blacks in Germany, a history that will be as necessary and important for those who come after us as it is for us today. When you have to struggle for your survival every day, it's not easy to do the work of making black history, the story of the black experience in Germany, visible. Oten the effort taxes us almost beyond the limits of our strength, but we're doing it anyway.

"The nationally organized Initiative of Black Germans and Blacks in Germany has grown. Every year our annual conference attracts greater numbers; above all, the numbers of black German children are on the increase. Throughout the year, we sponsor events, workshops and lectures on many themes, including how to search for one's parents, black literature and history, homosexuality, and much more. We share our experience of racism and the survival strategies we've each had to develop just to exist in our racist society. There's enormous interest in the workshops and lectures on black role models and heroes. Very few members of the black German community have ever been exposed to figures such as Martin Luther King, Jr., Malcolm X, Angela Davis, or the controversial Louis Farrakhan. We also try to present role models from closer to home, to provide context and orientation. I'd like to close these remarks by reading a few lines from Audre Lorde's poem 'Outlines' . . .

"we have chosen each other
and the edge of each other's battles
the war is the same
if we lose
someday women's blood will congeal
upon a dead planet
if we win
there is no telling."

In the intense, combative, almost hurtful discussion that follows, I'm hit ice cold in the face with these white women's resistance to anything demanding or uncomfortable. *There's so much violence against women in general; by contrast, many fewer women suffer from racism.* I ask myself once again how a movement like the women's movement can say that its mission is emancipation if it fails to address racism and anti-Semitism as well as sexism. I leave the room and go out to get some fresh air.

Sara Lennox, an old friend of Dagmar's, comes up to me. She's one of the few white women who raised her voice over the clamor to protect me from the others' sharp words. She puts her arms around me, even though she's hardly in any condition to soothe me herself. Later in the evening, she approaches me and suggests that she might help me try to find my father. A hopeless undertaking, I tell myself, but I go ahead and give her his name and 1946 address, anyway. She doesn't seem like the type who would give up easily—why not let her try? I'm not optimistic, but the desire to meet my father is still always there inside me, even now. After another ten days, Dagmar and I return home. Our trip is over, and we resume our everyday lives.

Soon after our return, I receive a teaching post at a university in Berlin. The topic of the seminar I will teach is identity. At the first class, I ask all the students in turn to say something about their identities and how they define themselves. I introduce myself as a black woman, but a white student interrupts me.

"You're not black, if you ask me. It would probably be a lot easier for you if you were. But your fate is to be neither black nor white, and thus every attempt at being one or the other leads to a crisis of identity."

I'm proud to call myself black, Afro-German, or black German, even when white Germans like you don't like it. No one but me has the right to define who I am. No one else can tell me if I have "the right" to call myself a black woman. I know all too well that whites have always been allowed to decide on which side of the line each particular Afro-German falls. Your words tell me I'm not black enough in your eyes, not African enough, I don't fit your "Negro" stereotype—or perhaps you'd be more comfortable if I said *black*. Well, I have learned to unify the two cultures—black and white—and so the real issue is how you as a white woman handle it. Black history is my history too, and in that I include the story of blacks in Africa, America, and Europe. I'm proud of African and African-American history and proud to be a part of it—it means that I have more than just a single reference point. You say *destiny*. If there is such a thing, then my destiny is this: to have as my homeland a country whose racist culture states, today just as it did in my childhood, that I don't exist. For that is what it means when people like yourself refuse to believe that someone who is German could be black.

A PHONE CALL from America: Gloria asks us to come to St. Croix as soon as possible. Audre is dying She's growing weaker by the day. We book a flight and two days later, Dagmar, our friend May Ayim, and I are there.

Audre lies quietly but her breath comes hard. Her lips no longer speak, but her eyes search desperately for words. Her lips pull back just a bit when she is happy, but the rest of her body no longer moves. She wants to die here on St. Croix, where the sun wraps its soft warm arms around her; here on St. Croix, where the people have made her at home in a way she never experienced elsewhere; here on St. Croix, where people have made her laugh, shared their everyday worries and invited her to barbecues and on fishing expeditions; here on St. Croix, where people care for and support one another, and share what they have. This is where she wants to die, here where she is completely secure and surrounded by happiness, joy, and love.

Audre can no longer speak, and I experience her deathbed silence as a challenge to come up with my own words, words that I will speak now and in the future, words that I must take responsibility for. She will not give me further answers, nor even gesture with her eyes to let me know how she feels. I wipe the dying sweat from her forehead and kiss her. Her hands are clammy and I warm them. Her eyes are wide open, and I watch tears and a hint of fear flow across her face.

How much she wanted to live on, and yet how dignified she is in dying. It took me a long time to muster the courage to ask Audre what it was like to know she would die, what it was like to take leave of the world. We were sitting together, and in response to my question, she took out some of her poems and read to me. That was her way of talking to me about death. Audre's breathing falters and grows uneven and heavy. Sometimes it halts altogether. She is not alone

Audre dies at midnight on November 17, 1992, dignified and prepared, in the midst of a circle of friends. ["To live a fulfilled life—for however long—the how and why must take priority."—A. L., Nov. 17, 1988, *The Cancer Journals.*]

Tribute—to You, Audre

And when the time came, Audre, you said, "That's the whole truth"; one of the first sentences you spoke in German. "That's the whole truth," as true as you are dead, as true as you live in me.
Many people had special relationships with you, and many believed they had a unique connection to you. I had neither the one nor the other. We just had a lot of fun with each other and often laughed at the same things. I never told you what you meant to me; it was clear already and therefore unburdensome.
I never gave you a poem, only a few lines, and even they were written in my miserable English.
We laughed. That was important.
And when the time came, we exchanged clothes. Audre, you wore my jogging suit, every day, and there was no longer any place where it was inappropriate. It was comfortable. That was all.
And when the time came, we sat down and talked, you in German, I in English, with a dictionary between us.

You loved the most difficult words: AUSEINANDERSET-ZUNG *(argument)*, BEGEISTERUNG *(enchantment)*, AUS-STRAHLUNG *(radiance)*, LEIDENSCHAFT *(passion)*, and, not least, MITTELGROSS *(medium sized)*, because you wanted to buy a medium sized fish for Gloria, who was arriving in Berlin from St. Croix the next day—not a large one nor a small one, but a medium sized fish is what you wanted to buy.

And when the time came, you told me stories of your childhood. You told me how you lost control of your first sled, crashed into a tree and broke your foot. Actually, we didn't leave anything out, neither important things nor seemingly unimportant.

And when the time came, the exhaustion grew more intense, too soon for you, too frightening, so we turned it into visions. We decided we would go jogging in the morning. And it didn't matter if we really did it. The jogging itself was not the source of energy—the mere thought of it was athletic enough.

And when the time came, your pain was more frequent, and you woke Dagmar and me in the night, you held my hand and felt bad for having disturbed us. I promised you long nights and you knew I would be there for you every one of them, even the last, until your death.

I loved you as much for your laugh as for your struggle. The last thing that mattered to you was to take for once, rather than to give.

Yes, you were singular—but so are we all. That's just what you always said and would still say now.

Your legacy will be carried on—by me and by all of the black people of the world. I miss you terribly. There are times when I feel the loss as a sharp, painful lump in my throat. But your passion still burns in my heart, where it will never be extinguished.

THE TELEPHONE WAKES me just as I'm falling back to sleep. It's probably Dagmar, calling one more time before she boards her flight. She's always doing that when she travels, having forgotten some important phone call or message or just wanting to say good-bye once again.

I pick up the receiver.

"Ika?"

"Sara?"

"Ika, I found your father!"

I leap up from the covers and take a deep breath. "No, it's impossible," I say. "No, really? How? Are you certain?"

"Ika, you won't believe it. I found him in the phone book. He was the only Eddie with 'ie.' "

I am out of my mind, then completely nonchalant, then once again stunned, as I pace back and forth in the room.

"Ika? Are you still there? Listen, I called him and asked if he'd been in Germany between 1945 and 1946 and whether he was stationed in a small town between Munich and Nuremberg. He said yes. Then I asked him if he ever lived at 4959 Prairie Avenue. He said, 'Yes, before we bought our house on Fifty-seventh Street.'

And then I told him he had a forty-six-year-old daughter in Germany."

Sara's words set my mind spinning. Part of me feels as awkward, clumsy, and inarticulate as a little child. Part of me is as drunk on this news as if some-one had poured an entire bottle of cognac down my

127

throat. And a part of me is numb, so that it seems my heart stands still. It feels as if I've become another person entirely, as if some long accustomed protective shield has been lowered or, perhaps, exploded into a thousand tiny shards. Then words leap through my throat and burst from my lips, words like *father, my father, my black father, he's alive, he's not dead, he lives, he lives, he lives.*

"He seemed like a very calm person," Sara says. "At least he gave that impression on the phone. He didn't sound all that surprised to hear from you— almost glad, in fact. I was totally shocked to hear him say, without hesitation, that he was sorry he couldn't manage a flight to Europe right now, but he'd be delighted if you'd write him and enclose pictures of you as a girl and your mother from the time when he knew her. Ika, I couldn't stay on the phone after that— I was crying so hard. I was just so happy to have found him. I called him again the next day—I was afraid he'd take it all back. He could so easily have said no, I have no daughter in Germany. I'm not the one you're looking for. But he didn't. I wouldn't say this if I weren't certain, but he's your father. I asked him how tall he was and told you you were tall and that he had every reason to be proud of his daughter."

I take down my father's address and phone number, hang up the phone and feel something indescribable rising within me.

It's very early morning but nevertheless I yell at the top of my lungs, "I found my father!" Then I sit at the window, where I never usually sit, especially not this time of day, and let my mind wander, asking questions and venturing answers. Will he fit my

128

image of a father—if I even have one? What will our first meeting be like? Will he like me? Then I start to call all my friends and tell them the news: Sara found my father.

And then I wait, impatiently, for Dagmar's call. Why didn't she forget anything this time that would make her call home right away? I can't bear to wait till tonight, when we've planned to talk. In the early morning light I head to the kitchen, not for breakfast or tea, but a glass of schnapps. Then I return to the phone, to call everyone else I know and tell them my unbelievable news. Is it possible, I wonder, that I'm just dreaming this, or is it real? And what about the possibility that Sara's wrong, and it's not him?

It's afternoon, and the May sun is high in the sky when Dagmar finally calls from the London airport.

"Dagmar, I don't know how to tell you—are you sitting down? Sit down if you can before I go on."

"What? Forget about that one. I'm standing right in the middle of the airport surrounded by people rushing to their gates, and there's a cleaning crew at work in here as well."

"But I mean it. I'm not just saying so."

"What is it? What happened? Tell me!"

"Sara found my father."

"No."

"Dagmar? Are you there?"

"Yes," she says and bursts into tears. One of the cleaning crew hands her a tissue. She tells me she's going to turn right around and come home, but I tell her not to.

"You'll be home in a couple of days , and I'll make it till then. Let's just talk on the phone a lot, okay?"

129

Last of all, late in the day, I call my mother. I ask her quite theoretically what she'd say if I found my father. "What can I say, Erika? He surely dead by now. Where would you look for him? And would it be such a big deal for you if you did find him?"

"Oh Mama, I have! Or Sara—I've told you about her—Sara actually tracked him down and then called to tell me."

"Really?"

We talk about how I feel, how happy I am, but say not a word about how she feels. We hang up, but then a half an hour later she calls back.

"I really am so happy you've found him. I'd like to fly up to Berlin and take you shopping. We'll get you all the loveliest things so you can look your best when you meet him. But Erika, are you sure it's really him?"

I'm not really prepared for the question. What could I say, anyway, that I'm not sure? I don't let myself think about that possibility.

I can't sleep that first night. Everything inside me has shifted.

When I was a girl, I used to imagine that my father would ring the doorbell one day and take me away with him, it didn't matter where. In kindergarten I saw other children's fathers take them lovingly in their arms, and I would turn around and pose as if I were waiting for my father too. Each day I built up my fantasy and every day I grew more miserable, knowing that he'd never come and I'd never get to be close to him. Sometimes I thought I spotted him, but in fact I was only looking into the white faces of strangers, men who didn't even deign to look my way. My arms would hang limp at my sides, but I had

130

to struggle to suppress the urge to go up and embrace any old father, whether he was mine or not. I never gave up that dream of finding my father and going to him. I never gave it up, even when my girlfriends all said things like: *Oh, those Negro soldiers, they're all the same—they go around making babies and then vanish. When you try to find them, they deny responsibility because they're afraid you'll want money—alimony, child support, you know.*

"Allow me to give you one piece of advice: give up on this endless searching, for your own sake. Even if you found him, you'd only be disappointed. You already know he wants nothing to do with you. If he did, don't you think he would have found you himself? Men like that are worried only about holding onto their money."

"I just don't get why women are always searching for their lost fathers. I wouldn't have missed mine. He was a drunk and an arrogant pig. Why do we always have to place such a high value on men?"

Words like these infest my thoughts, and I can't get beyond them. Over and over again I'm hit with the fear that my father will turn out to be the man my friends have predicted. I want to see him anyway, though. Just once. I know so very little about him. Where is he from? Where and how did he grow up? How old is he? Has he been loved in his life? Is he married? Are his parents, my grandparents, still alive? Is it possible I have siblings? Aunts and uncles? Cousins? Does he remember anything of his time in Germany with my mother? Did he ever love her? Like her? How long did they actually know each other? What did he look like then, and now? I will write him a letter, my second, and this one will arrive.

131

Perhaps I wouldn't feel so helpless in all this if I hadn't been systematically stripped of all ability to access my own feelings as a child. Perhaps, otherwise, I wouldn't awaken deep in the night groping for words to express what moves me most deeply. It is now within my reach to have a father. Getting up and going to bed, I have the same feeling, as if I were a schoolgirl writing my first letter and frightened of making an error.

When I finally bring myself to sit down with paper and pen, I'm at a loss for how to begin. My courage leaves me with the very first decision: how to address him. *Dear Dad? Dear Father? My Dear Father? Hello Dad?*

In the next four days I begin forty-two letters and even come close to finishing a few. I read each one over, and every time I rip it up and toss it in the trash. I pace through out the apartment brooding over my words. They must be just the right words, and they must capture feelings that are indescribable, these words for the most important letter of my life.

> Hello,
> It's not easy to write this letter. (I am typing to make sure you can read it well).
>
> On the one hand, I am overjoyed to finally know that you are alive and where you live. On the other hand it is very strange to find my father late in my life—as it must be for you to hear that you have a daughter in Germany. So I want to tell you a bit about myself.
>
> I was born on March 13, 1947, in . . . My mother tried to find you, but she got a letter from the

Police Department of Chicago saying that no one by that name lived at that address (I enclose a copy of the letter). The only photo she had of you my stepfather tore up, and I never could see it. There seemed to be no way to find you— I did not even think of the most obvious, the telephone book. My friend Sara Lennox, who called you and who knew how important it was for me to find out something about you, finally had that idea.

Before I moved to Berlin in 1990, I lived in Frankfurt for twenty years. I studied at the School for Social Work, and then I worked in a home for youths. Now I am responsible for publicity and presswork in a small publishing house. I have published some articles myself.

I am a joyful person although you can imagine it is not easy to live here in Germany with a different skin color. But I have fought until today to maintain my human dignity. I am proud to be black, but it was a long way to feeling that. Even though I did not know you, it has been the color of my skin which has always connected me with you. In 1990, I took my exam as a black belt in Tae Kwon Do in Columbus, Ohio. My trainer in Frankfurt comes from the U.S. That was my first visit to the United States. The following year and since then I have been in the U.S. every year visiting friends. In 1991, I spent two days in Chicago. I thought of you there and even had in mind to check out your old address. But it happened that our whole luggage was stolen shortly after our arrival, and my friend and I spent all day getting tickets etc. replaced. This August, we will again go to the U.S.

Sara Lennox sent you a copy of my talk I gave when I was invited last year to tell German teachers something about the situation of Afro-Germans.

There is a lot more I could tell you about me, as you can imagine. When I was very small, some friends of my mother, who knew you, said that I looked like you. I don't know if that is still so. I am sending some childhood photos and a couple of recent ones, as well as two old photos of my mother. Of course, I have been waiting for so long to see you.

I don't know what it is like for you to suddenly hear you have a grown up daughter whom you don't have to worry about and can be proud of. I, in any case, am very happy that you are alive and hope that you are well and have had persons around you who love you. I could keep on writing—it feels like you are sitting opposite me. But I will end here and send you my very best wishes hoping very much to hear from you.

Your daughter

Days and weeks go by. When the mailman hands me a stack of mail, I can barely look. All sorts of letters arrive, every sort except the one from my father.

Everyday I grow more agitated and yet somehow also calmer, sadder, less certain. *Maybe you shouldn't have sent the letter by registered mail. Maybe he was afraid it was something official and didn't want to pick it up.* Of course. That's it. But why did I ask anyone else's opinion? Why didn't I hide my fear? The next few days are unbearable. I drag myself straight home after work, collapse in the armchair and am overcome by sobs. Finally I decide to send Gloria a fax in St. Croix, asking her to call him and find out whether he received my letter. I don't have to courage to do it myself.

"Is it Wednesday?" I ask Dagmar tiredly. It is, and I've completely forgotten that this is the day I have my English class. I glance in the mirror and determine that I look awful, but what does it matter? On my way downstairs, I decide to walk rather than to ride my bike. The evening is mild. I swing my handbag over my shoulder, trying to muster courage. He will write me, he must write me, I insist that he write me. I see a clock and realize I'm a half an hour late. The class is small—just five women and two men. "Finally," whispers my friend Gisela. "It's about time. Do you have your homework? We're just going over the translation. But what's going on with you—did someone die?"

"Spare me," I say and decide to get up and go. I don't belong here tonight. Back at home, I sink exhausted into the chair by the telephone and hide my face in my hands. I'm sure now that I'll never hear from my father. I'm filled with doubt.

The phone rings. I jump to answer it, then look down at it in fear.

"Dagmar, you answer it. I just can't. I'm too worked up."

I hear her say, "Gloria, is that you?"

135

Impatiently, I shift my weight from foot to foot and understand nothing Dagmar's saying—it's as if all my knowledge of English has just flown out my head. But then I get fragments: "He got it . . . a week later . . . the son's having pictures copied . . . a southern accent . . . I believe that . . . she talks a lot . . . very nice . . . Ika will be happy . . . what? sending it tomorrow . . . maybe next Friday . . . we'll see you next week then . . . when does your plane get in . . . okay, I'll tell her, good bye." A letter from my brother, my father and my step mother will be coming next week. I take a deep breath, and it's as if I haven't breathed in a long, long time. I throw my arms around Dagmar.

On July 25, 1993, at half past noon, exactly one week after Dagmar's call, I receive the much awaited letter.

> Hi Ika,
> I received a phone call from your friend Sara Lennox. She informed me I have a daughter in Germany who is trying to locate me. She asked if I was in Germany in 1946, in the Air Force and a town stationed near . . . I said yes, and that's when I heard of you. This revelation made me very happy.
>
> After leaving Germany, I arrived in Chicago just before Thanksgiving, November 1946. My wife stayed at 4959 Prairie Avenue. Soon after my arrival we moved to 43rd and Indiana Street. Your mother got my address from a friend I worked with on station. We would list our address on a going away board, where my wife's address was listed. Just before I left Germany,

your mother told me she was pregnant. Soon after that, I became ill with the hives and was admitted to the hospital for a week. I was released and sent back home to the States without seeing or hearing from her again. Ika, please forgive me, but I forgot your mother's name after all these years. I am 75 years of age in fairly good health. I have a loving wife and family, two girls and three boys, all grown up now. Looking at your pictures, you in the infant stroller favored me when I was a child. Plainly, you have my nose. I am looking forward to seeing you.

Your Dad.*

I don't normally jump for joy or sing praises to the heavens, but it wasn't an ordinary day

Dear father,
I am sure you can imagine how excited I was to get your letter. It was even more exciting to finally see what my father looks like. You are right, I resemble you very much, more than I thought. I am proud to look like you. Your letter moved me, and I am glad about your openness. Thank you.

Of course, I am very excited about meeting you and perhaps your other children. Today I received the ticket for my trip to the U.S. I will visit Gloria Joseph in St. Croix together with my friend. (Gloria is in Berlin at the moment and staying with me.)

* Abridged.

137

Gloria talked to your wife on the phone and liked her very much. I am looking forward to meeting both of you. We will arrive in Chicago on August 20 at 3:40 P.M., and I will call you as soon as I have arrived at the house of friends. On August 23, we will go on to St. Croix.

Is there anything I could bring you from Germany? I would like to fulfill you any wishes you might have.

I haven't called you because my English is not so good, and I am afraid that I would not find words on the phone. But when I see you in August, I am sure we will find ways to communicate. I understand more English than I speak.

Many greetings to your wife and children. I am so happy to see you soon! Take care.

Your daughter Ika

It is high summer and hot outside. A group of friends is driving Dagmar and me to the airport. In the car, Nina rubs my neck and tells me stories about plane crashes and doors falling off, but laughingly tells me she loves to fly anyway.

"Thanks a lot," I tell her.

"Relax," says Beate. "Nothing's going to happen to the plane." But I'm not worried by the teasing. Nothing can bother me. The fact that in seven or eight hours I will be landing, hopefully safely, in my father's city puts me in the mood to laugh along with them. Giggling and joking like a bunch of teenagers, we arrive at the airport with enough time for all of us to sit down together for a farewell cup of coffee before the flight. It's hot and humid. Just thirty-five minutes, I think. And then Dagmar and I say good-bye to them, clasping hands and hugging.

"Good luck!" they call as we move through the security check. "We'll be thinking of you. Remember Ika, you've got nothing to lose and everything to gain."

"Ladies and gentlemen, for security reasons, our flight will be departing a few minutes later than scheduled. Please fasten your seatbelts and remain in your seats until the captain has turned off the overhead fasten-seatbelt signs."

My heart pounds. I'm suddenly terrified of dying. I swallow hard and sit bolt upright until the bell chimes and a voice comes over the speakers again. "This is your captain speaking. We apologize for the delay. We had a piece of luggage on board whose owner we couldn't identify, but it's been cleared up and we'll be leaving the gate in about five minutes." At least that one source of tension has been eliminated. I lean back in my seat, page through magazines, listen to music, but I'm still incredibly agitated. I munch continually on pretzels and cookies and drink soda, bloody Mary mix, orange juice, tea. There's no chance I'll get any sleep. First I'm too cold, then too hot. Dagmar tries to soothe me by reading aloud to me and stroking my head, but also understands that this state of agitation will be quelled in only one way. I look at my watch—just an hour to go until Dagmar's old friend Bea will pick us up at the airport in Chicago. "Please bring you seat backs and tray tables to the upright position," blares from the overhead speakers.

139

"We will be landing in Chicago shortly. We hope you have enjoyed your flight and that you'll chose to fly with us again the next time you travel. The captain and his crew wish you a pleasant and productive stay in Chicago or wherever your final destination may be."

Dagmar and I are waiting for our luggage when suddenly a new reason to panic occurs to me: what if all our bags don't arrive? All the new clothes my mother bought for me are in one suitcase, and without them I'd be lost. After all, we picked them out specially for this visit. But at least I have the gifts for my family in my carry-on. For my father, there are framed photos of me. For my stepmother, Corene, I have a silk shawl, and for my sisters, Deloris and Linda, and my brothers, Larry, Eddie Jr., and Gregory, I've had T-shirts printed up with drawings of my own design. A quarter hour later, we leave the baggage area with all of our things. Crowds of people are standing just beyond the arrivals area, eagerly awaiting their relatives or friends. Bea is nowhere in sight, though. She's still not there when eventually the crowd has dispersed. Three quarters of an hour later, I'm close to tears and we decide to have Bea paged. Without result—she still doesn't show up. I say a few quick prayers and start to look for her myself. I've only seen her in pictures, but somehow I'm sure I'll recognize her. Scarcely ten minutes later, I spot a short, slim, blonde woman some two hundred yards away. She has a big bag over her shoulder and hurries toward us.

"Oh God, finally I've found you! Welcome to Chicago. Dagmar, you haven't changed a bit—we're just a little older. Can you imagine: the terminal was changed and it took me forty-five minutes to figure out where to find you. But I'm here now. How are

140

you, Ika? What a day this is for you. Let me give you a hug."

All I can think is how much time I'll have to rest up from the flight before we turn around again—and set out to meet my father.

"You should by all means see your father alone. It's the most important moment of your life, after all. Think about it!"

I have thought about it, a long time, and the more I do so, the sadder and more uncertain I become. Instead of happiness or excitement, I'm feeling fear. Fear of this strange country, fear of this foreign language (not to mention the dialect of Black English on top of that). Fear of meeting with my father for the first time at forty-six years of age. It's too much all at once, too much for me to handle. It was a few weeks ago, after talking with May Ayim, that I decided I wanted to take Dagmar with me.

"Ika, take along the person who's closest to you, whom you trust and who will stand by you when your feelings and your heart are out of control. They're going to be, you know—or at least mine were when I met my father. I still wish I'd had a friend along with me. I cried for weeks afterward."

Glencoe lies on the outskirts of Chicago. It's a white neighborhood like something out of a picture book, and Bea lives here. The single family homes lie like toy houses along the shores of Lake Michigan. Every house has a beautiful front yard filled with shrubs and flower beds. White lace curtains hang in all the windows. This could be the fanciest neighborhood in Berlin, the only difference being that here people greet me on the street as if they knew me.

141

In a whirlwind I run a damp washcloth over my face, change my clothes, drink a quick cup of coffee and rush off with Dagmar to catch the train that will take us to my father. It departs the station with a high-pitched whistle. There are a few other blacks in the car, but otherwise it could be any train, anywhere. Then the conductor's announcement proves that we really are in the U.S. "This train stops at Hubbard Woods, Winnetka, Indiana Hill, Kenilworth, Wilmette, Central Street, Evanston, Main Street, Rogers Street, Ravenswood, Clybourn, and Chicago. Next stop, Hubbard Woods."

I've stopped thinking or feeling. I'm functioning. Functioning the way one must when one has sur-passed the limits of one's courage, strength, expecta-tions, longing, and ability to hope, to feel, or to think.

"Chicago."

Dagmar and I exit the train and find a pay phone. I pick up the receiver and struggle to tell Corene in my best English that we'll be there in about a half an hour: "We will come in thirty minutes. We take a cab," is the best I can manage. She babbles at me, a stream of words, none of which I understand, and I simply say over and again: "We will come in thirty minutes. We take a cab."

"West Fifty-seventh Street, please," Dagmar says to the black cab driver. I say nothing. As we drive through the city, my heart beats faster and faster.

"The U.S.—the entire country is a piece of crap. I wouldn't live there if my life depended on it. How can anyone there like fast food—ketchup and hamburgers. Grim. The culture is in a state of total decay. Have you ever been over there? You won't get me to make that trip." Why, of all things, do these glowing endorsements

142

have to be on my mind right now? People see exactly what they want to see, as I well know. I take deep breaths and try to calm myself.

"You sure you want to go to West Fifty-seventh," asks the cabby, emphasizing the word *west*. He looks back at us disbelievingly through the Plexiglas.

"Yes, West Fifty-seventh," repeats Dagmar. The neighborhoods grow shabbier and shabbier. We've left the imposing architecture behind us, though this area bustles with just as much life as the downtown. The houses are grayer and the people less well dressed and there are increasingly more blacks.

"You're *sure* you want to go to West Fifty-seventh."

Dagmar repeats herself again, in case he simply hasn't understood her, but there's no chance it's Dagmar's English that's the problem here. She lived in the States for ten years, and studied and taught here. Her English is excellent.

"I just want to be sure you didn't confuse South for West."

Dagmar takes my hand. I lean back and pray silently that this man is taking us to the right street. We veer off to the right.

"Because West Fifty-seventh—that's an all black neighborhood."

"Yes, sir, we are absolutely sure."

Soon the taxi slows, makes a sharp left and turns onto West Fifty-seventh.

"Here we are," he says, stopping in front of a small driveway.

My Father

My father
just a few steps more
I get out of the car
both our first steps
we come closer
for the first time now

A shy glance
a timid smile
I've never seen you laugh

Tears but just for the blink of an eye
Tears that take me home

We come closer
late
and beyond the limits of time

As for you, you welcome me
As for me, a dream of longing is fulfilled

You climb the steps silently
smile when you see me
I go cautiously to your side

Voices startle me
the door opens
I look into black faces
the table is laid

I reach out my hand
to my black family
my father, my family
here is my journey's end
here the whole world comes together

Every hour, every minute, every second with my family is full of warmth and love. I am overwhelmed by the unrestrained welcome and also by the fact that Dagmar, as a white woman, is also accepted by my family. These feelings are somewhat subdued by my exhaustion, however. My father smiles cautiously. Our eyes meet again and again. I see similarities between us that are so remarkable it makes me dizzy. We don't talk a lot, because words could not begin to express what we're feeling. Corene brings out photo albums and shows me my aunts and uncles, my nieces and nephews. All of them are black. Only on one page do I find a single white face: my mother's. So even she has been included in this family album. I am more than moved. I blush deeply. I'm encountering human kindness and love here the likes of which I've never experienced before.

I wonder if such a meeting as this would be possible in my country. If Afro-Germans who were adopted and raised in the U.S. would receive a comparable welcome. I think of Rose.

Once, when we were on vacation in St. Croix, I got a call from a friend. "Ika," she said. "I've met a woman who's searching for her white German birth mother. She'd really like to meet you." That afternoon, I visited her. Her full name was Rosemarie, and from the age of three she grew up on St. Croix with black adoptive parents and a brother, another adopted black child. On the table between us lay her forty-year-old adoption papers and several photo albums. Rose didn't remember any German at all and was curious to hear her mother tongue spoken. It was exhilarating for both of us: she who spoke my father tongue; I who spoke her mother tongue; I who had searched for my father; she who was searching for her mother. We turned the album pages to picture after picture of black faces—father, mother, extended family, friends. It moved me. It was only fairly recently that I'd first been able to add some black faces to my own album full of white faces. Rose was happy not to have grown up in Germany and told me she'd been shocked when she read the German book *Showing Our Colors*. "I'm a little scared of finding my mother," she told me. I understood her. We felt a bond, and I saw for the first time that it might be even more difficult to look for a mother than a father.

I'm still immersed in thought of Rose when Larry calls us to sit down at the lavishly spread table, saying I must be hungry after the long journey. From time to time, my father seems to notice I'm hot and adjusts the fan. I don't have to do a thing—it seems they anticipate my every wish, just by looking in my eyes. I sit here in the lap of my black family, and am made to feel at home as I never have before. I am my father's first and oldest daughter. Deloris is eight months younger, and then come Larry, Linda, Gregory and, last, Eddie, Jr. Every one of my siblings notices some particular resemblance between my father and me. I look most like him of all the children. Linda says I have his mouth and chin. Larry sees an unmistakable similarity in our gestures. Deloris notices my fingernails are shaped like his, and Gregory is struck to see how my ears and nose are just the same shape as my fathers'. There's no question that I am his child.

Suddenly I'm reminded of the letter from my father in which he described himself as having been a brilliant dancer, once, and talked of how he was

146

involved in starting up dance clubs all over the U.S. Larry puts on a tape. Jazz and soul bring the room alive, and dancing is in the air, along with contentment, the rhythms of life and the fact that I am here, in the midst of my black family. I'm exhausted. Never in my life have I been quite this tired. I'm desperate for some rest. Before going back down the front steps of my family's house, I turn around once more, thinking to give my father a kiss of farewell, but then I can't bring myself to do it. My sisters Linda and Deloris drive us to the station. I dream of my father that night, my seventy-six-year-old father, this wise old man, my father. His hair is gray and his life has been hard and full of sorrow but also filled with love and the joy of being alive.

MY FATHER LIES gravely ill in a bed in the intensive-care unit, and I am there beside him. I don't want him to die. Not now—I've only just found him. Will these be the only hours I spend alone with him? He promises me that he will endorse my application for American citizenship. That will be his legacy to me. There's nothing more he can do for me, but he wants to leave me something.

He takes my hand gently, takes a deep breath and looks at me peacefully. Both of us are shaky. There is a certainty in his love for me—it's active, unmistakable, indestructible. He's holding my hand in one of his, and the other rests on my shoulder. I'm right there with him, yet he's moving away.

When I look into his eyes, they tell me, "Don't be afraid. I'm your father. Please know that I would never do anything to hurt you. We just have to get used to each other." But how much time will we have to do that? Will it be enough? I smile. He smiles, and something incredibly human passes between us. I watch him sit up with difficulty and know there's nothing I can do to make him well again. God knows I would give anything to keep him from dying. I want to pull the covers up over his shoulder—I can see he's cold—but I don't have the courage to do it. I struggle to fight back my tears; and to assure him that I'll always take good care of myself. I tell him that if he must die, at least we have this hour. I will never forget it—nor will he. I'll carry it in my heart the rest of my life.

Visiting hours are over, and I have to leave. I'm going back to Germany. He wishes me a safe trip, and

149

I promise that I'll be back. A few weeks later, he's released from the hospital, but his health doesn't improve. He sounds exhausted and sad when we talk on the phone.

I knew it, of course—we both suspected it—but now it seems certain we won't see each other again. I comfort myself by remembering over and over his voice saying "I love you, honey." I imagine what it would be like if we could walk the streets of Chicago or Berlin together, what it would be like to look out at the world while walking proudly beside my father.

My father dies on May 6, 1994.

> To my family and to my father,
> I'm very sorry not to be able to mourn Dad's death together with you all. Yet, even though I am in Berlin, thousands of miles away, my heart and my love are still with you.
>
> I certainly cannot imagine the whole extent of what Dad's loss means to you— your loss of a life partner, dear Corene, and yours of your father, my sisters and brothers. But I can feel how sad you are. I am sorry, and my heart is heavy, too.
>
> To you, my family, I want to say:
> You met me with love and trust, and this trust made me very happy.
>
> To you, Corene, I want to say:
> You are a wonderful woman and mother. There was no reason for you to take me into your heart in such a loving way. I admire your

strength, your generosity and your humanity—
a humanity which never existed in the country
I live in. I wish you a lot of support in this time.
Your life may not always have been easy, but
you have many good memories of a person
who meant so much to you and will always
mean a lot to you.

To you, my sisters and brothers, I want to say:
Even though we have had very little time
together, you have made me feel so welcome.
Rarely in my life have people looked forward
to meeting me as much as you have. I have
known primarily the white society, have
grown up within it as an outsider, as someone
who does not belong. I did not know you, and
when I came to you on August 20, 1993, you all
made me feel that I belong to you. I am with
you in my thoughts, accompany you in these
days and in the coming times. I wish you
strength and that the pain will not be too bad.
I am with you.

Dear Dad, to you who decided that you wanted
to pass, to rest, I want to say:
I love you. You know, it isn't how long people
know each other, but what they have to say and
give to each other that matters. Certainly, I have
just found you, learned to love you, and it was
not much time we had together, but enough to
know you took me into your heart as you did
your other children. You understood how much
I needed you. You knew how much I longed to
get to know my black father. For forty-six years,

151

I had fought against being destroyed by white people, not to let them take my humanity away.

I found you, and I was compensated for all the humiliation and struggles.
I found you, and I knew that my survival in a white racist society was not for nothing.
I found you, and I felt that what whites say about Blacks is not true and only serves to oppress us.
I found you, and I felt stronger in doing my part to force white society to give us the respect we deserve.
I found you, and was full of fears and caution.
You stretched out your hand and put your heart around me.
Meeting you healed me and gave me strength to walk straight and with pride though this world.
I found you, and I will never lose you again.

Now you can rest, and longed-for peace will be with you for all time. I keep you deep in my heart. You have the space in my life which rightfully belongs to you. Farewell on your passage. We will see each other again, when- and wherever it may be.
Your daughter Ika who will always love you.

It's time. I pack up my documents for the U.S. Consulate in a transparent plastic folder and carefully place them in my briefcase. I hope I haven't forgotten anything. It is my first visit there.

Before I could start on this trip, I waited weeks for the original copy of the declaration of paternity, which Larry had sent by Express Mail. The declaration of paternity, which was much more important to me than American citizenship, which I wanted the way I'd wanted my father, never arrived. I waited for months for a notarized copy of the original. Finally I received a copy of my father's birth certificate, but this was insufficient. As with the paternity declaration, I had to have the original documents. Which was impossible, as the building in Louisiana where the records were stored had been burned down years before. Again, I waited weeks for a replacement. Offices I wrote to were no longer at the addresses I'd been given, and it took me a lot of time and effort to find the new ones. Without Sara Lennox's help, I would never have managed it all.

It was a long, painful process. Especially painful because all the documents brought me closer to my father. I learned, for example, from one of the documents, that he only reached the fourth-grade level. At that time, four years of school were quite a lot for black people, who had no right to an education. The whites needed them to work in the cotton fields. My father was born in 1917 in Delta, Louisiana. His father, my grandfather, worked on the railroads. He left Louisiana in 1927 and settled with his family in Marigold, Mississippi. My grandfather died in 1941. My grandmother died in 1979 at the age of ninety-six, having outlived her husband by thirty-eight years.

So many things run through my head when I hold these papers of my father's in my hands. Mississippi— a state of poverty, of slavery, of oppression, of the fight for civil rights. In Mississippi, they told the lives and destiny of black people by singing the blues. I would

153

like to have talked to him about his time in Mississippi. I would have liked to go there with him.

It takes two years for me to gather all the documents, and when I finally have them, the trip to the consulate is not an easy one to make.

On June 11, 1996, it happens: I'm granted American citizenship. My father would have been overjoyed to hear the news. But he left me a family, brothers and sisters, and they celebrate with me from afar.

A half year after I receive my U.S. passport, I locate Rose's mother.

Epilogue

June 15, 1997. The feeling of returning, after thirty-five years, to the place I spent my childhood is indescribable. Little has changed except that there's a parking lot in the yard where I once was made to pull weeds.

How large this place loomed in my memories, and how small, how unimpressive, it is now before me. Quietly, sunk in my own thoughts, I look around me and also within myself. I begin to re-envision moments from my life here, but time and again, I must stop. I can't bear to think the memory through to the end. I feel a crushing pain in my heart, and for a long moment I feel totally cut off from life.

There are children playing in front of the building, and they greet me in a friendly manner. They're at home here, living with foster parents who love them. I don't stop to talk to them but watch, from a distance. They laugh and play and act quite naturally, something I wish I could say of myself at this moment.

As much as I am comforted by the sight of these laughing children's faces, I'm also saddened. I feel abandoned. I'm sorry there's no one left here to ask me for forgiveness.

I take leave afresh from my childhood.

I was seven years old when my mother left me alone at the home, and it hurt me infinitely. I never really learned to bear being away from home, where I was safe, where I belonged. I was panicky and fearful the whole way there, to the home. I was afraid I would never come home again. I never did, except on and off for the holidays. That pain is a lifelong one.

Sometimes, especially when I'm traveling, I can picture myself as a child, holding the hand of my mother. Sometimes I catch myself staring at trains. long trains that are taking people away and bringing them home, people who board and disembark, some of whom will never return, just as I never did.

Today, my mother is seventy-two years old and her curly brown hair is run through with gray. We have both grown older, leading our separate lives. Memories remain. It hurt to be sent away from her and to exchange security for physical and psychological violence. But even today, it's hard for me to be angry with my mother. She's the only one in the world who truly belongs to me, who is with me, even now.

I have long since forgiven her, and she has long since asked for my forgiveness.

Although my birth brought unspeakable humiliation upon my mother, I remember feeling nothing negative—not being hit, not being treated dismissively, not being unloved. She did not send me away to the home because of any shortage of love for me.

How could I sustain anger at the one person who stood by me always, even if it was from a distance? Sometimes I marvel at the hostility friends of mine feel toward their mothers and fathers. I respect it. But I could never endure such rage. I needed to have at least one person whose love I was sure of, and that was my mother. My mother loves me, and I am her daughter, forever. My confidence in my mother's love is what enabled my survival in this racist society, and it continues to bring me that assurance. My mother and I

156

both know all about the pain that resides within both of us and about the love that binds us.

My sister Lisa is forty-eight years old now. She has dark brown hair and has been married since the age of twenty-four. She has a twenty-one-year-old son and a seventeen-year-old daughter.

Much to my surprise, Lisa came to Berlin a few days before my fiftieth birthday. She helped with preparations for the party and got to know many of my friends. She was especially glad to meet other Afro-German women—for I was the only one she'd ever known. One night when we were eating dinner with a small group of friends, a remarkable discussion took place. One of my white friends asked Lisa what it had been like to have a black sister, what experiences she remembered, how she had felt. And for the first time, Lisa spoke about this subject which had been unmentionable. I held my breath. Lisa hesitated at first. She was afraid that what she said would hurt me and she didn't want to cause me pain. But she also believed that this was the time and the place to say it, while I was in a supportive group of close friends. She talked about how painful it had been for her to deal with the jeers and insults of her in-laws concerning me and my mother. How much she had had to put up with and how even her children had been affected. She had no one she could share this with. She couldn't talk to her friends about it, or with her mother, only in a very limited way with her husband, and not at all with me. She said that she too was branded as the daughter of a nigger whore, and that she had often been reminded of it by people she knew and by her husband's family. She told us that her wedding and reception had almost been canceled because they

157

learned she had invited me. She talked about how often she'd been reminded of our mother's "conduct," sometimes subtly, sometimes directly. She talked about how long she had had to hold in her rage, her feelings of helplessness and her grief and how conflicted she had been. Her only comfort, she said, was the unconditional love of her children.

I was glad and relieved to learn at last about her anger and her sorrow and that she was afraid of hurting me with her feelings, even if it was rather late in coming. Lisa and I had never in all those years been able to tolerate each other's anger, much less express it. That night we moved a step closer.

Although I was able to talk about my childhood experiences with my Afro-German and white friends, that kind of openness between Lisa and I had been impossible. But now we can begin. Lisa and I will have many conversations, and I cannot imagine having a better sister.

I have everything today: my life, my longings, my love, a light-hearted happiness, humor, respect, and pride in myself. Every morning, I look forward to the coming day and experience the world anew. I look in the mirror and am happy, for there's nothing in the world I want to be but myself.